Cisco Networking Academy Program
IT Essentials I: PC Hardware and Software Lab Companion

Cisco Systems, Inc.
Cisco Networking Academy Program

Cisco Press

201 West 103rd Street
Indianapolis, IN 46290 USA

Cisco Networking Academy Program
IT Essentials I: PC Hardware and Software Lab Companion

Cisco Systems, Inc.
Cisco Networking Academy Program

Course Sponsored by Hewlett-Packard Company

Copyright © 2003 Cisco Systems, Inc.

Published by:
Cisco Press
210 West 103rd Street
Indianapolis, IN 46290 USA

Printed in the United States of America   1 2 3 4 5 6 7 8 9 0

First Printing   January 2003

ISBN: 1-58713-094-7

Warning and Disclaimer

This book is designed to provide information about PC and Hardware setup, configuration, and troubleshooting. Every effort has been made to make this book as complete and as accurate as possible, but no warranty or fitness is implied.

The information is provided on an "as is" basis. The author, Cisco Press, and Cisco Systems, Inc. shall have neither liability nor responsibility to any person or entity with respect to any loss or damages arising from the information contained in this book or from the use of the programs that may accompany it.

The opinions expressed in this book belong to the author and are not necessarily those of Cisco Systems, Inc.

 This book is part of the Cisco Networking Academy Program series from Cisco Press. The products in this series support and complement the Cisco Networking Academy Program curriculum. If you are using this book outside the Networking Academy program, then you are not preparing with a Cisco trained and authorized Networking Academy provider.

For information on the Cisco Networking Academy Program or to locate a Networking Academy, please visit www.cisco.com/edu.

Trademark Acknowledgments

All terms mentioned in this book that are known to be trademarks or service marks have been appropriately capitalized. Cisco Press or Cisco Systems, Inc. cannot attest to the accuracy of this information. Use of a term in this book should not be regarded as affecting the validity of any trademark or service mark.

The logo of the CompTIA Authorized Curriculum Program and the status of this or other training material as "Authorized" under the CompTIA Authorized Curriculum Program signifies that, in CompTIA's opinion, such training material covers the content of the CompTIA's related certification exam. CompTIA has not reviewed or approved the accuracy of the contents of this training material and specifically disclaims any warranties of merchantability or fitness for a particular purpose. CompTIA makes no guarantee concerning the success of persons using any such "Authorized" or other training material in order to prepare for any CompTIA certification exam.

Feedback Information

At Cisco Press, our goal is to create in-depth technical books of the highest quality and value. Each book is crafted with care and precision, undergoing rigorous development that involves the unique expertise of members of the professional technical community.

Readers' feedback is a natural continuation of this process. If you have any comments regarding how we could improve the quality of this book, or otherwise alter it to better suit your needs, you can contact us at networkingacademy@ciscopress.com. Please be sure to include the book title and ISBN in your message.

We greatly appreciate your assistance.

Publisher	John Wait
Editor-in-Chief	John Kane
Executive Editor	Carl Lindholm
Cisco Representative	Anthony Wolfenden
Cisco Press Program Manager	Sonia Torres Chavez
Cisco Marketing Communications Manager	Tom Geitner
Cisco Marketing Program Manager	Edie Quiroz
Production Manager	Patrick Kanouse
Development Editor	Christopher Cleveland
Project Editor	San Dee Phillips
Technical Editors	Jim Drennen, Arthur Toch, Arthur Tucker
Copy Editor	Cris Mattison

Corporate Headquarters
Cisco Systems, Inc.
170 West Tasman Drive
San Jose, CA 95134-1706
USA
http://www.cisco.com
Tel: 408 526-4000
    800 553-NETS (6387)
Fax: 408 526-4100

European Headquarters
Cisco Systems Europe
11 Rue Camille Desmoulins
92782 Issy-les-Moulineaux
Cedex 9
France
http://www-europe.cisco.com
Tel: 33 1 58 04 60 00
Fax: 33 1 58 04 61 00

Americas Headquarters
Cisco Systems, Inc.
170 West Tasman Drive
San Jose, CA 95134-1706
USA
http://www.cisco.com
Tel: 408 526-7660
Fax: 408 527-0883

Asia Pacific Headquarters
Cisco Systems Australia,
Pty., Ltd
Level 17, 99 Walker Street
North Sydney
NSW 2059 Australia
http://www.cisco.com
Tel: +61 2 8448 7100
Fax: +61 2 9957 4350

Cisco Systems has more than 200 offices in the following countries. Addresses, phone numbers, and fax numbers are listed on the Cisco Web site at www.cisco.com/go/offices

Argentina • Australia • Austria • Belgium • Brazil • Bulgaria • Canada • Chile • China • Colombia • Costa Rica • Croatia • Czech Republic • Denmark • Dubai, UAE • Finland • France • Germany • Greece • Hong Kong • Hungary • India • Indonesia • Ireland Israel • Italy • Japan • Korea • Luxembourg • Malaysia • Mexico • The Netherlands • New Zealand • Norway • Peru • Philippines Poland • Portugal • Puerto Rico • Romania • Russia • Saudi Arabia • Scotland • Singapore • Slovakia • Slovenia • South Africa • Spain Sweden • Switzerland • Taiwan • Thailand • Turkey • Ukraine • United Kingdom • United States • Venezuela • Vietnam • Zimbabwe

Table of Contents

Introduction

The *IT Essentials I: PC Hardware and Software Lab Companion* supplements the online course and the companion guide. It provides hands-on experience along with review questions to support the material covered. This book is useful in its own right as a hardware and software basics lab manual. The easy-to-follow exercises are useful when the goal is to pass the A+ Certification and to continue with IT Essentials II: Network Operating Systems.

The topics covered in the book include the internal components of a computer used to successfully assemble a system, installing an operating system, and troubleshooting using system tools and diagnostic software. Also, you work with architectures to connect to the Internet and to share resources in a network environment.

You will find that your studies are best complemented by a text that describes the theory and foundational concepts introduced in the hands-on lab exercises. To that end, the Cisco Press *IT Essentials I: PC Hardware and Software Companion Guide* includes thorough treatments of the topics discussed in this lab manual.

Who Should Read This Book

This book is intended for the student in high school, technical school, community college, or a four-year institution who wants to pursue a career in IT Technology or who wants to have the working knowledge of how a computer works, how to assemble a computer, and how to troubleshoot hardware and software issues.

This Book's Organization

This book is divided into chapters corresponding to the chapters in the companion guide:

- Chapter 1-Labs and worksheets include Windows basics and number conversions including binary, decimal, and hexadecimal, and lab safety.

- Chapter 2-Labs and worksheets that identify the internal components of a computer including the motherboard, ROM and BIOS chips, video card, and power supply.

- Chapter 3-This chapter focuses on assembling a computer system. The labs provide hands-on experience for connecting the power supply, motherboard, and drives.

- Chapter 4-The operating system is installed in this chapter. The worksheets focus on the fundamentals and navigation, and the labs deal with DOS and creating a boot disk.

- Chapter 5-The worksheets provide a review of the Windows file system, managing printers, and hard drive preparation. The labs actually prepare the hard drive and install the operating system. Troubleshooting skills include installing drivers and creating a Windows startup disk.

- Chapter 6-Multimedia is the focus of this chapter. The labs and worksheets include both sound and video. You install a sound card and update the video card. Additionally, you review the terminology as it relates to CDs and DVDs.

- Chapter 7-In this chapter, the differences between Windows 9x and Windows 2000 are detailed. The labs demonstrate the upgrade to Windows 2000 and the steps to create an emergency startup disk.

- Chapter 8-The worksheets in this chapter review the concepts of RAID and the steps to add a processor to a server and to upgrade a server adapter.

- Chapter 9-Networking is detailed in this chapter. The network interface card (NIC) is installed and configured in the labs, plus you troubleshoot by using the PING command. The worksheets review the types of networks and topology, and connecting to the Internet.

- Chapter 10-In this chapter, you complete labs to manage files in a printer queue and to allow print sharing. The worksheet provides the information required to clear a paper jam.

- Chapter 11-The labs in this chapter focus on preventive maintenance including using a digital multimeter, cleaning computer components, and using system tools. Environmental issues, ESD, and general preventive maintenance are covered in the worksheets.

- Chapter 12-Troubleshooting basics are covered in this chapter. The labs cover the steps of the troubleshooting cycle and identifying POST errors. The worksheets cover troubleshooting printers and hardware in general.

- Chapter 13-Troubleshooting as it relates to software is the focus of this chapter. In the labs, you boot to the Safe Mode, use the Windows 2000 Recovery Console, and back up the Windows Registry.

This Book's Features

This book contains several elements that help you learn about the basics of hardware and software for the PC:

- Objectives and Scenarios-Each of the labs in this manual provide an objective or a goal of the lab. The equipment required is listed, and a scenario is provided that allows you to relate the exercise to real-world environments.

- Reflection Questions-To demonstrate an understanding of the concepts covered, a reflection question is provided at the end of the lab. Also, questions are included that are designed to elicit particular points of understanding. These questions help verify your comprehension of the technology being implemented.

The conventions that present command syntax in this book are the same conventions used in the Cisco IOS Command Reference:

- Bold indicates commands and keywords that are entered literally as shown. In examples (not syntax), bold indicates user input (for example, a show command).

- Italic indicates arguments for which you supply values.

- Braces ({ }) indicate a required element.

- Square brackets ([ ]) indicate an optional element.

- Vertical bars (|) separate alternative, mutually exclusive elements.

- Braces and vertical bars within square brackets (such as [x {y | z}]) indicate a required choice within an optional element. You do not need to enter what is in the brackets, but if you do, you have some required choices in the braces.

CompTIA Authorized Quality Curriculum

The contents of this training material were created for the CompTIA A+ Certification exam covering CompTIA certification exam objectives that were current as of December 2002.

How to Become CompTIA Certified

This training material can help you prepare for and pass a related CompTIA certification exam or exams. In order to achieve CompTIA certification, you must register for and pass a CompTIA certification exam or exams.

In order to become CompTIA certified, you must

1. Select a certification exam provider. For more information, please visit http://www.comptia.org/certification/general_information/test_locations.asp.
2. Register for and schedule a time to take the CompTIA certification exam(s) at a convenient location.
3. Read and sign the Candidate Agreement, which will be presented at the time of the exam(s). The text of the Candidate Agreement can be found at http://www.comptia.org/certification/general_information/candidate_agreement.asp.
4. Take and pass the CompTIA certification exam(s).

For more information about CompTIA's certifications, such as their industry acceptance, benefits, or program news, please visit http://www.comptia.org/certification/default.asp.

CompTIA is a nonprofit information technology (IT) trade association. CompTIA's certifications are designed by subject matter experts from across the IT industry. Each CompTIA certification is vendor-neutral, covers multiple technologies, and requires demonstration of skills and knowledge widely sought after by the IT industry.

To contact CompTIA with any questions or comments:
Please call + 1 630 268 1818
questions@comptia.org

Lab 1.3.8: Getting to Know Windows

Estimated Time: 10 Minutes

Objective

Upon completion of this lab, you will have been introduced to the proper way of shutting down Windows and navigating the Windows interface, and to using Windows Help features.

Equipment

The following equipment is required for this exercise:

- Lab computer with Windows 98 installed

Scenario

To help a friend with Windows, you need to be more familiar with the Windows graphical user interface (GUI).

Procedures

Knowing how to use the Windows interface can help you in nearly any job today. The majority of computers that are in the work place have a version of Windows installed on them. To work in a Windows environment, you need to have a firm grasp of the following skills: resizing windows; creating and deleting icons, files, and folders; and navigating the **Start** button (Shutdown, Run, Search, Settings, Documents, and Programs).

Step 1

If your lab computer is not already on, boot it up. If you are prompted for a login name and password when Windows has booted, use the username and password assigned by your instructor.

Step 2

At the Windows desktop, become familiar with the Windows interface to make troubleshooting faster and easier. Take a minute to click the **Start** button and look through the items listed in the Start menu.

What options are listed under the Find menu?

_____

_____

Step 3

Try running the Calculator program by selecting **Start** > **Programs** > **Accessories** > **Calculator**. Enter a few simple test calculations to see how it works. Try using both the mouse and the numeric keypad. When finished, click the **X** on the top right corner of the Calculator program to close it.

Step 4

Now try the help system that is built into Windows. Help is organized in books and includes a search feature so that you can quickly locate specific topics. To begin, click the **Start** button and click **Help**. This opens a window with a list of categories that outline the major areas that Help covers.

Click the **Search** tab and enter one or more words relating to the topic that needs research. Do a search for the word "resize."

After completing a search for "resize," what topics does Help display?

_____

_____

There is also an **Index** tab, which lists all Help items alphabetically.

Step 5

There are different ways of resizing a window to minimize or maximize. If you want to see more of a help item in one screen, you can resize the window. The fastest way to view a window in full screen is to click the **Maximize** button. The maximize button is the middle button on the top right corner of the window.

To return the window to its original size, click the **Restore** button. The Restore button replaces the Maximize button when the window is in full screen.

To resize the window to a custom size, grab the edges or corners of a window first by moving the mouse cursor to the edge or corner of the window. When the double-arrow appears, click and hold the mouse button and drag the window to the desired size.

Step 6

To properly shut down Windows, click the **Start** button and select **Shutdown** from the menu. Select **Shutdown** from the list and click the **OK** button. The computer should always be shut down using this method. Important data that is stored in memory while the system is running needs to be written to the hard disk before turning off the computer. Do not turn the computer off until a message displays indicating that it is safe to do so. Newer operating systems automatically turn off power when the shutdown process is complete. The power button should be used only to turn the computer on.

Troubleshooting

The Windows Help feature is a valuable tool when the technician needs information on a specific topic. If there is something in Windows that you need to research, using the Help feature can answer many questions.

Reflection

What is the proper way to shut down Windows?

_____

_____

Why is it important to shut down Windows properly instead of just pressing the power button?

_____

_____

Lab 1.5.3: Boolean Operations

Estimated Time: 25 Minutes

Objective

Upon completion of this lab, you will have been introduced to the AND, OR, NOR, and NOT Boolean operations. You will also be able to calculate the output of combinations of Boolean operations based on input.

Equipment

This is a written exercise.

Scenario

You are given a circuit board diagram. To figure out what each logic gate does, you must understand how Boolean operations function.

Procedures

This lab helps you learn to work with Boolean operations. Computers use Boolean operations to make calculations based on inputs of 0 (OFF) and 1 (ON). 0s and 1s are represented in computer microchips and the bus on the motherboard by the presence or absence of voltage. You will perform some basic calculations using the AND, OR, NOR, and NOT Boolean operations to get a better feel for how computers work internally. Complex combinations of these operations take place all the time in computers — these calculations occur in millionths of a second.

Step 1

The Boolean operations of AND, OR, NOR, and NOT work as follows:

0 OR 0 is 0	0 AND 0 is 0	0 NOR 0 is 1	NOT 0 is 1
0 OR 1 is 1	0 AND 1 is 0	0 NOR 1 is 0	NOT 1 is 0
1 OR 0 is 1	1 AND 0 is 0	1 NOR 0 is 0	
1 OR 1 is 1	1 AND 1 is 1	1 NOR 1 is 0	

The corresponding truth tables allow a compact way to represent these operations:

	0	1		AND	0	1		NOR	0	1
0	0	1		0	0	0		0	1	0
1	1	1		1	0	1		1	0	0

Note: AND, OR, and NOR are called binary operations (not to be confused with binary numbers) because the operations require two inputs. NOT is called a unary operation because it has only one input. Look at the following combination of Boolean operations and determine the output.

(1 AND 0) OR (0 AND 1)

Compute the operations in parentheses first. 1 AND 0 is 0. 0 AND 1 is 0. So the solution is 0 OR 0, which is 0.

As a second example, try to compute the following Boolean operations.

NOT [(1 AND 0) NOR (0 OR 1)] AND 1

Work from the inner parentheses toward the outer parentheses. Also, the NOT applies to the expression that follows it. (The NOT does not apply to anything that appears after the].) So, following these instructions, you get NOT [0 NOR 1] AND 1, which is equivalent to NOT [0] AND 1, which is the same as 1 AND 1. This gives the result of 1.

Step 2

For each of the following combinations of Boolean operations, compute the final output based on the rules for AND, OR, NOR, and NOT. Refer to the preceding truth tables for help on how to compute any given Boolean operation.

Solve for the output. Your answer should be a 0 or a 1.

Input: NOT (1 AND 0) AND 1

Output: _____

Input: 1 NOR {NOT [0 OR (1 NOR 1)]}

Output: _____

Input: 0 AND {1 AND [1 OR (0 NOR 0)] AND 0} —you have to work left to right through the expression.

Output: _____

Input: 1 AND NOT {[0 OR (1 OR 0)] NOR [1 AND NOT (0)]}

Output: _____

Troubleshooting

As a PC technician, understanding how data is stored in a computer can be a great troubleshooting tool.

Reflection

How are Boolean operations used in computer systems?

_____

_____

Lab 1.5.9: Converting Numbers Overview

Estimated Time: 25 Minutes

Objective

Upon completion of this lab, you will be able to identify the places in binary and decimal numbers and know the value of each. Also, you will work with powers of 10 and relate them to decimal places, and work with powers of 2 and relate them to binary places. Finally, you will manually convert between simple binary numbers and decimal numbers and describe the differences between binary and decimal number systems.

Equipment

This is a written lab exercise.

Scenario

Having sharp skills in number systems can aid you in your career as an IT professional. With the ability to convert numbers without the use of a calculator, you can solve problems that might arise quickly and easily.

Procedures

This lab helps you learn to work with the binary number system. You will convert binary numbers (Base 2) to decimal numbers (Base 10) and then from decimal to binary. Computers and networking equipment, such as routers, use binary numbers, a series of binary digits (bits) that are either ON (a binary 1) or OFF (a binary 0). They are encoded internally in the PC on microchips and on the computer motherboard's bus as electrical voltages. Understanding binary numbers and how they relate to decimal numbers is critical to understanding how computers work internally.

Step 1

The decimal number system is based on powers of 10. This exercise helps you develop and understand how the decimal number system is constructed. With Base 10, the right-most place has a value of 1 (as with Base 2). Each place moving to the left is valued 10 times more. Therefore, 10 to the zero power is one ($10^0 = 1$), 10 to the first power is 10 ($10^1 = 10$), 10 to the second power is 100 ($10^2 = 10 \times 10 = 100$), 10 to the third power is 1000 ($10^3 = 1000$), and so on. Just multiply the number in each place with the value of each place (for example, $400 = 4 \times 10^2 = 4 \times 100$). Remember that any number (other than 0) to the zero power is 1.

The following chart shows how the decimal number system represents the number 352,481. This helps in understanding the binary number system:

Exponent	10^5	10^4	10^3	10^2	10^1	10^0
Expanded	100000	10000	1000	100	10	1
Place Value	3	5	2	4	8	1
	3 x 100,000	5 x 10,000	2 x 1000	4 x 100	8 x 10	1 x 1

The number 352,481, if read from left to right in expanded decimal form, is (3 x 100,000) + (5 x 10,000) + (2 x 1000) + (4 x 100) + (8 x 10) + (1 x 1), for a total of 352,481 (a six-digit number).

Here is another way to look at it that makes it easier to add up the decimal number values:

Position of Digit (from Right)	Value of Bit Position (10^X or Ten to the Power Of)	Number Value from 0 to 9	Calculation	Decimal Value
1st Decimal Digit	10^0 or 1	1	1 x 1	1
2nd Decimal Digit	10^1 or 10	8	8 x 10	80
3rd Decimal Digit	10^2 or 100	4	4 x 100	400
4th Decimal Digit	10^3 or 1000	2	2 x 1000	2000
5th Decimal Digit	10^4 or 10,000	5	5 x 10,000	52,000
6th Decimal Digit	10^5 or 100,000	3	3 x 100,000	300,000
Decimal Value (Total of 6 Digits)				352,481

Step 2

Binary means two and each digit in a binary number can have only two values (0 or 1). Binary numbers are key to understanding how computers work. The value of each binary digit, or bit, is based on powers of two.

This exercise helps develop an understanding of powers of two, which is what all computers and data communications use. With Base 2, the right-most place has a value of 1, as with Base 10. Each place moving to the left is valued two times more. Therefore, 2 to the zero power is one ($2^0 = 1$), 2 to the first power is 2 ($2^1 = 2$), 2 to the second power is 4 ($2^2 = 4$), 2 to the third power is 8 ($2^3 = 2$), and so on. Just multiply the number in each place (either a 0 or a 1) by the value of each place (e.g., $8 = 2^3 = 1 \times 8$) and add up the total. Remember that any number (except 0) to the zero power is 1.

Binary Number Conversion Example

The following table shows the detailed calculations (starting from the right side) to convert the binary number 10011100 into a decimal number:

Position of Digit (from Right)	Value of Bit Position (Two to the Power Of)	Is Bit a 1 (ON) or a 0 (OFF)	Calculation	Decimal Value
1st Binary Digit	$2^0 = 1$	0	0 x 1	0
2nd Binary Digit	$2^1 = 2$	0	0 x 2	0
3rd Binary Digit	$2^2 = 4$	1	1 x 4	4
4th Binary Digit	$2^3 = 8$	1	1 x 8	8
5th Binary Digit	$2^4 = 16$	1	1 x 16	16
6th Binary Digit	$2^5 = 32$	0	0 x 32	0
7th Binary Digit	$2^6 = 64$	0	0 x 64	0
8th Binary Digit	$2^7 = 128$	1	1 x 128	128
Decimal Value (Total of 8 Bits)				**156**

Step 3

Look at the binary number bit status. If there is a 1 in a given position, add the value shown. If there is a 0 in a given position, do not add it.

Solve for the decimal value.

Exponent	2^7	2^6	2^5	2^4	2^3	2^2	2^1	2^0
Bit Position	8	7	6	5	4	3	2	1
Value	128	64	32	16	8	4	2	1
Binary Number Bit	1	0	0	1	1	1	0	0

Decimal Value:

_____

Exponent	2^7	2^6	2^5	2^4	2^3	2^2	2^1	2^0
Bit Position	8	7	6	5	4	3	2	1
Value	128	64	32	16	8	4	2	1
Binary Number Bit Status	1	1	1	0	0	0	1	1

Decimal Value:

_____

Exponent	2^7	2^6	2^5	2^4	2^3	2^2	2^1	2^0
Bit Position	8	7	6	5	4	3	2	1
Value	128	64	32	16	8	4	2	1
Binary Number Bit Status	0	1	1	1	0	0	0	0

Decimal Value:

_____

Exponent	2^7	2^6	2^5	2^4	2^3	2^2	2^1	2^0
Bit Position	8	7	6	5	4	3	2	1
Value	128	64	32	16	8	4	2	1
Binary Number Bit Status	1	1	0	1	1	0	1	0

Decimal Value:

_____

Step 4

Convert the decimal values of 209, 114, 58, and 165 to their binary equivalents. To do this, look at the decimal value and subtract binary values starting from 128 (the highest value binary bit for these numbers). If the number is larger than 128, put a 1 in the 128 (or 2^7) column. Subtract 128 from the number and see if there is 64 or greater left over. If there is, put a 1 there; otherwise, put a 0 and see if there is 32 or greater left over. Continue until all 8 bits are defined as either a 0 or a 1.

Exponent	2^7	2^6	2^5	2^4	2^3	2^2	2^1	2^0
Bit Position	8	7	6	5	4	3	2	1
Value	128	64	32	16	8	4	2	1
Binary Number Bit Status								

Binary Value of 209:

_____

Exponent	2^7	2^6	2^5	2^4	2^3	2^2	2^1	2^0
Bit Position	8	7	6	5	4	3	2	1
Value	128	64	32	16	8	4	2	1
Binary Number Bit Status								

Binary Value of 114:

_____

Exponent	2^7	2^6	2^5	2^4	2^3	2^2	2^1	2^0
Bit Position	8	7	6	5	4	3	2	1
Value	128	64	32	16	8	4	2	1
Binary Number Bit Status								

Binary Value of 58:

_____

Exponent	2^7	2^6	2^5	2^4	2^3	2^2	2^1	2^0
Bit Position	8	7	6	5	4	3	2	1
Value	128	64	32	16	8	4	2	1
Binary Number Bit Status								

Binary Value of 165:

_____

Step 5

Check your answers by converting the numbers back.

Troubleshooting

Learning how to calculate binary numbers without the use of a calculator is an important skill in the IT industry. The ability to perform number conversions can save time, especially in the field where calculators are not always available.

Reflection

Using the system that you learned to solve decimal to binary conversion, convert the decimal number 255 to binary?

_____

_____

_____

Worksheet 1.3.8: Windows Navigation and Settings

1. It is extremely important not to power off the computer using the _____.

2. The main display screen in Windows is known as the _____.

3. The _____ contains the Start button, quick launch buttons, and the clock.

4. The _____ menu allows you to access virtually every program and function on the PC.

5. To adjust the date and time, double-click the _____ on the right side of the _____.

6. Most applications have three tiny icons in the upper right corner of the screen that _____ the screen, _____ the screen, or _____ the application.

7. To adjust the screen display, first _____ all windows that are open. Right-click empty space on the _____ and choose Properties.

8. To access the volume control, click the _____ icon on the right side of the _____.

9. To move a desktop icon to another position on the desktop, click it and _____ it to the desired location.

10. After it is highlighted, you can rename icons, like folders, by clicking the _____ and typing in a new one.

11. To create a new folder, _____ the desktop and select **New** > **Folder**.

12. The _____ bar displays the name of the document and application.

13. The _____ bar contains menus for manipulating the document, such as creating new documents, copying text, inserting images, and so on.

14. The _____ bar shows useful information, such as page number, whether the file is being saved, how to access the Help feature, and so on.

15. The _____ bars appear when the document is too large for it to fit on the screen and can move the image or text through the window.

Worksheet 1.5.9: Number Systems Exercises

1. Define the following:

Decimal: _____

_____

Binary: _____

_____

Hexadecimal: _____

_____

2. Explain how binary and hexadecimal numbers are used with computers:

_____

_____

_____

_____

_____

_____

_____

_____

3. Without using a calculator, convert the binary numbers into decimal numbers.

A. 01111011 _____   B. 00000111 _____

C. 11110000 _____   D. 10101010 _____

E. 01010101 _____   F. 10010011 _____

G. 00111001 _____   H. 11111111 _____

I. 11010101 _____   J. 10000000 _____

4. Convert the decimal numbers into binary numbers.

A. 23 _____   B. 131 _____

C. 3 _____   D. 234 _____

E. 79 _____   F. 199 _____

5. Convert the decimal numbers into hexadecimal numbers.

A. 16 _____   B. 131 _____

C. 3 _____   D. 234 _____

E. 65 _____   F. 255 _____

6. Convert the hexadecimal numbers into decimal numbers.

A. 27 _____   B. AA _____

C. 3 _____   D. F1 _____

E. 241 _____   F. 255 _____

Worksheet 1.6.6: Lab Safety Checklist

Fill in the blanks in the following lines:

1. The workspace for an IT technician should be large enough to accommodate the following:

   a. _____

   b. _____

   c. _____

   d. _____

   Near the workbench, power outlets should be available to at least accommodate the system unit power and the power needs of other electrical devices.

2. The workspace should maintain a humidity level of _____ percent to reduce the likelihood of electrostatic discharge (ESD).

3. The workbench should be a _____ surface; additionally, it should have a flat cleanable surface.

4. The workspace should be distant from areas of heavy _____ equipment or concentrations of _____.

5. The workspace should be free of_____ .

   _____can contaminate the workspace, causing premature damage to computer components.

   The work area should have a filtered air system to reduce _____ and contaminants.

6. Lighting should be adequate to see small details. Two different illumination forms are preferred: an adjustable _____ with a shade and _____ lighting.

7. Extreme variations of _____ can affect a computer's components. _____ should be maintained, which is consistent with the components' specifications.

8. Properly AC electrical current is essential. Power outlets should be tested with an outlet tester for proper grounding.

Lab 2.3.2: Motherboard Identification

Estimated Time: 30 Minutes

Objective

This lab focuses on your ability to identify motherboards, remove motherboards, replace motherboards, and use motherboard manuals to identify a number of the system's components.

Equipment

The following equipment is required for this exercise:

- A system board (either mounted in a case or not)
- Internet access
- Motherboard manuals
- ID software or local vendor contact

Scenario

You have just been hired by a PC repair center and have started your training. PC technicians need to be able to remove and replace motherboards either in an upgrade situation or because of a motherboard failure.

Procedures

If the system board has been diagnosed as needing replacement, a few guidelines must be followed. Place the system on an antistatic mat and use an antistatic wrist strap. Verify that the system's power cord is not attached.

All necessary safety precautions need to be followed carefully concerning power supplies and electrostatic discharge.

Step 1

Gain access to the motherboard. If the motherboard is installed in a case, remove the case cover.

Step 2

If needed, remove components and cabling to gain access to the motherboard manufacturer's name and ID number. Be sure to carefully record these connections so that they can be properly replaced.

Note: these numbers might not be easily read, so look carefully. As you become familiar with different manufacturers, it gets easier.

Because of variations in motherboards, not all the following information might be available. On others, additional information might be available. Check with the instructor about your system.

Step 3

Record the following information from the computer's motherboard:

Components	Available? (Y/N)	Name/Type (if applicable)
1. Motherboard Manufacturer	Y	SiEMQSS
2. Motherboard Model Number	Y	U-ATX - MAINBOARD SILLS
3. Form Factor (physical size and layout)	Y	Micro-ATX 9.6"x8"
4. Type of CPU Installed	Y	iNTEL PENTiUM II
5. Types of CPUs Supported (socket or slot)	Y	PentiUM II/III or CELERON/slot
6. Chipset	Y	INTEL 82440 BX, PiI X4 E
7. BIOS Manufacturer	Y	PHoNiOX NuBIOS V6.0G
8. BIOS Battery	Y	MAXELL CR2032
9. ISA or EISA (number and type)	Y	1
10. PCI (number and type)	Y	3
11. AGP or AGP Pro (number and type)	Y	1
12. Jumpers	Y	1 MY1-15
13. DIP Settings	Y	

Troubleshooting

A quick check on the motherboard manufacturer's web site provides information regarding the motherboard BIOS and whether an upgrade is available.

Reflection

The ability to properly identify all the components of a motherboard will prove to be useful when troubleshooting in the field.

Where is the first place to look to determine the manufacturer of a motherboard?

_____

_____

Lab 2.3.4: Identify ROM and BIOS Chips

Estimated Time: 30 Minutes

Objective

This lab focuses on your ability to locate and identify the ROM chip, BIOS chip, and BIOS manufacturer on your motherboard.

Equipment

The following equipment is required for this exercise:

- A complete motherboard
- Motherboard manuals
- Internet access for research

Note: A functioning system is not necessary to complete this lab. Be sure to observe proper care concerning power supplies and electrostatic discharge (ESD).

Scenario

A client that you built a PC for a few months ago recently purchased a used computer. He wants to install an expansion card into the machine to add some video editing capabilities. Before he purchases an expansion card, he wants to make sure that the BIOS will support it.

Procedures

BIOS—The Basic Input/Output System is a ROM chip that has built-in commands that allow the system to power up and perform a self-test of its hardware before turning over control to the operating system.

ROM—Read-only memory, as its name implies, can be read, but not changed. It stores basic information that the computer needs to operate (for example, the BIOS).

Determine the manufacturer and version number of the BIOS. Research the BIOS manufacturer's web site to see newer versions are available. Also, examine the physical ROM chip to help answer the following questions.

Step 1

Describe the physical appearance of the ROM chip and its location on the board:

_____

_____

_____

Step 2

What type of BIOS is used?

Manufacturer:	
Version/Type:	
Battery Type:	
Rewritable?	

Step 3

If an Internet connection is available, visit the manufacture's web site and list the version number and any new features that are supported.

_____

_____

_____

Step 4

Can the BIOS be upgraded?

_____

_____

_____

Step 5

What are the steps you take to upgrade the BIOS?

_____

_____

_____

_____

Troubleshooting

Use extreme caution when flashing the BIOS. Make sure it is the correct file and that it is not corrupt. If you flash your BIOS with the incorrect BIOS type or with a corrupt file, you can render the board inoperable!

Reflection

How many BIOS manufacturer's can you list?

_____

_____

_____

_____

Why is the BIOS needed?

_____

_____

_____

_____

Lab 2.3.5: Identifying Computer Expansion Slots

Estimated Time: 20 Minutes

Objective

Upon completion of this lab, you will be able to identify safety issues, specifications, and components relating to expansion slots. You will also be able to list the advantages and disadvantages of each expansion slot.

Equipment

The following equipment is required for this exercise:

- Motherboard and motherboard manuals
- Expansion cards (not required, but additive)
- Internet access for research

Scenario

Bob purchased a used computer and is trying to determine what type of video card and other expansion cards can be installed. Help Bob figure out what is currently installed so that he can make an educated decision when he is ready to buy new expansion cards.

Procedures

An expansion slot is a long, thin, socket connection located on a motherboard or riser board that allows various cards to be added to a computer. These cards can include devices such as modems, sound cards, and network interface cards (NICs). Expansion slots allow the life of a computer to be extended because new technology can be added as it becomes available.

Verify that the power cord is disconnected and that the antistatic wrist strap is in place. Remove the computer's system case.

Step 1

Locate the expansion slots on the motherboard (or riser card) and list them:

1	4.
2.	5.
3.	6.

Step 2

Using your resources, identify any expansion cards that are installed:

1.	4.
2.	5.
3.	6.

Troubleshooting

Occasionally when a PC is shipped from one location to another, an expansion card can become unseated. Verify that all expansion cards are properly seated and that all connectors are properly plugged in before turning the unit on.

Reflection

What type of expansion cards are installed in a PCI slot?

_____

_____

_____

_____

What is the speed difference between PCI and ISA expansion slots?

_____

_____

_____

_____

Lab 2.3.7: Identifying RAM and RAM Sockets

Estimated Time: 40 Minutes

Objective

This lab focuses on the identification of various types of RAM and RAM sockets.

Equipment

The following equipment is required for this exercise:

- A functioning computer system with two dual in-line memory modules (DIMMS) installed.

- The proper tools to remove the computer's cover.

- Manual for the motherboard used in the computer.

- (Optional) RAM tester. If you are unsure of the operation of the RAM tester, ask the instructor for further instruction.

Scenario

Fred wants to upgrade the amount of RAM in his PC but is not sure how to locate it or how to determine how much RAM is installed. Help him to determine what he has so that he can figure out how much more to buy.

Procedure

Random-access memory (RAM) is memory that the CPU uses to store open files and active applications temporarily. RAM is volatile, meaning that any information stored in it is lost when powered-down. RAM comes in small expansion board forms with varying numbers of edge connectors. The RAM sticks are made in 30, 72, 168, or 184 pin configurations. They are referred to as single in-line memory modules (SIMMs) or DIMMs—depending on the chip density. Many times, the only information to be gained visually is the manufacturer's name. This is why a quality RAM tester is a critical piece of diagnostic equipment for PC repair shops.

Observe proper care concerning power supplies and ESD.

Step 1

Boot your system and record the power-on self test (POST) amount of RAM:

_____

Step 2

Shut down your system and follow all the safety steps in removing the computer's cover.

Step 3

After gaining access to the motherboard, note the position of the RAM slots and whether they are in use, making notes in your journal.

SLOT TYPE:	
TOTAL NUMBER OF SLOTS:	
NUMBER OF SLOTS OPEN:	
TOTAL RAM CAPACITY:	

Step 4

Record the information about the installed RAM sticks in the following table.

MANUFACTURER:	
TYPE:	
CAPACITY: (each)	
SPEED:	
TOTAL CAPACITY INSTALLED:	
POSITION:	

Step 5

Refer to the motherboard manual or search the Internet for the type and range of RAM chips that can be installed on this computer.

Step 6

If there are two sticks of RAM installed, remove one of your RAM sticks, noting the location and orientation of the stick.

Step 7

Replace the computer's cover and plug in the power cords. Restart the computer system. Note the POST RAM amount. _____

Step 8

Shut down the system and follow all the safety steps in removing the computer's cover.

Step 9

Replace the RAM stick that you removed in Step 6.

Step 10

Replace the computer's cover and plug in the power cords. Restart the computer system. Note the POST Ram amount. _____

Step 11

Reflect in your journal about any special considerations that you should be aware of as you install the RAM memory.

Attach copies of any additional research material used in completing this worksheet before handing in this assignment.

Troubleshooting

Take extreme caution when working with RAM. ESD is one of the most prevalent problems when working on computers. Make sure that you have an antistatic wrist strap on at all times and that you are properly grounded. The chips on a RAM module are built for 3.3 volts. If a static discharge is large enough for you to see a spark, it is 3000 volts.

Reflection

Did you use an antistatic wrist strap the entire time you were working with the RAM modules?

_____

What other types of RAM are there besides the type installed in the PC you worked on?

_____

Lab 2.3.9: Video Card Identification

Estimated Time: 35 Minutes

Objective

The major features and specifications of different video cards are discussed in this lab. You will be able to identify the video card by any markings on the card. These include a manufacturer's name and part number. Some cards might be identified only by the physical layout of the card.

Equipment

The following equipment is required for this exercise:

- ESD wrist strap
- Standard tool kit
- Lab workstation with AGP video card installed
- Internet access
- Manufacturer manuals

Scenario

You are an avid gamer and want to compare the features of all the video cards at your disposal. Because you need the latest and greatest video card for the latest and greatest games, you need to pay special attention to the manufacturer and performance specifications of each video card.

Procedures

A video adapter, or card, is an expansion card that allows the computer to display images on a monitor. It also determines the monitor's depth and resolution. The need for the video card is determined by the intended usage of the system. For example, a system used for gaming needs a much higher end card than one used for word processing.

Step 1

After removing the system case, remove the video card from its expansion slot. When working with video cards, similar to any other component on the inside of a computer, take special care to be grounded and make sure to use an antistatic wrist strap. If the video card is damaged, the computer will be useless until a new video card is installed.

Research and supply the following information:

Manufacturer:	
Model number:	
URL site:	
Key features:	
System requirements:	
Cost:	

Terms

Research the following terms using the following Internet resources and other Internet resources:

- www.techweb.com/encyclopedia
- www.webopedia.com/

AGP port:

_____

_____

_____

_____

EDO RAM:

_____

_____

_____

_____

Pixel:

_____

_____

_____

_____

Refresh rate:

_____

_____

_____

Resolution:

_____

_____

_____

Troubleshooting

When working with video cards, similar to any other component on the inside of a computer, take special care to be grounded and make sure to use an antistatic wrist strap. If the video card is damaged, the computer will be useless until a new video card is installed.

Reflection

Did any of the video cards work without having a heat sink or a fan on the graphics processing unit (GPU)?

_____

_____

Are video cards with a heat sink or fan on the GPU available?

_____

_____

Why would having a separate processor on a video card help performance?

_____

_____

_____

Worksheet 2.3.1: PC Power Supply

1. The most basic function of the PC power supply is to convert _____ current to _____ current.

2. What is the purpose of the cover panels?

   _____

   _____

3. What are some factors to consider when purchasing a computer case?

   a. _____

   b. _____

   c. _____

   d. _____

   e. _____

   f. _____

   g. _____

4. In Europe, the standard outlet delivers_____Volts AC, and in North America, the standard wall outlet delivers _____ Volts AC.

5. What rating do computer power supplies have? _____

6. What are the two most common power supply types?

   a. _____ b. _____

7. What is the importance of the power supply fan?

   _____

   _____

   _____

   _____

Worksheet 2.3.4: BIOS/ROM

1. The BIOS serves as the interface between the _____ and

   the _____.

2. The detailed instructions needed for system start-up are stored in _____.

3. BIOS stands for _____.

4. ROM stands for _____.

5. What special characteristic do EPROM, EEPROM, and Flash ROM have?

   _____

   _____

   _____

   _____

   _____

   _____

6. What differentiates RAM from ROM?

   _____

   _____

   _____

   _____

   _____

Worksheet 2.3.5: Expansion Slots

1. What are expansion slots? _____

2. An expansion bus is also referred to as a (an) _____

   or _____.

3. An expansion bus is used to add _____ to existing systems.

4. List five different types of expansion slots:

   a. _____

   b. _____

   c. _____

   d. _____

   e. _____

5. Define Plug and Play:

   _____

   _____

   _____

6. Name three common types of expansion cards:

   a. _____

   b. _____

   c. _____

7. Name the three bus types:

   a. _____

   b. _____

   c. _____

8. An ISA bus was developed with both _____ bit and _____ bit bus speeds.

9. Which bus type supports bidirectional communication? _____

   _____

10. What does PCI stand for? _____

Worksheet 2.3.7: RAM and RAM Sockets

1. Memory chips in a computer system are referred to as _____.

2. RAM is the industry standard abbreviation for _____.

3. Define volatile as it applies to RAM:

_____

_____

4. Name the two basic types of RAM:

a. _____

b. _____

5. Which type of RAM needs to be re-energized constantly to retain its contents?

_____

6. Define RAM parity:

_____

_____

7. _____ refers to the process by which the computer

rewrites data to RAM.

8. Describe the physical difference between a SIMM and DIMM chip:

_____

_____

_____

_____

9. Define memory caching:

_____

_____

_____

_____

Worksheet 2.3.9: Video Cards

1. A video card converts a _____ signal into a _____ signal.

2. Video cards are also known as _____ or_____.

3. The video card receives its data from the _____and sends it to the_____.

4. _____ provides video during bootup until the necessary video drivers can take over.

5. The abbreviation CRT stands for_____.

6. List the three colors mixed together within the CRT to produce all other colors:

   a. _____

   b. _____

   c. _____

7. How closely the pixels are grouped, which translates to how sharp the picture appears, is referred to as _____.

8. VGA and SVGA video adapters use a standard _____-pin connector to connect to the monitor.

9. The term pixel stands for _____.

10. The term VGA stands for _____.

Worksheet 2.3.13: Floppy Drive

1. Explain what a floppy drive is used for in a computer:

_____

_____

2. Define the following parts of a floppy disk drive:

   Motor: _____

   _____

   Stepper Motor: _____

   _____

   Read/Write heads: _____

   _____

   Photosensitive diode: _____

   _____

   Floppy drive circuit board: _____

   _____

3. How are floppy drives categorized?

_____

_____

4. List the different parts of a floppy disk:

   a. _____

   b. _____

   c. _____

   d. _____

5. What are the two most common sizes of floppy disk drives?

   a. _____

6. List the different data rates at which floppy drives operate.

    a. _____

    b. _____

    c. _____

    d. _____

7. List the common storage capacities found on a floppy disk:

    a. _____

    b. _____

8. What type of coating is found on a floppy disk? _____

9. When a floppy disk is formatted, how is it organized? _____ and

    _____.

10. How many tracks are found on a 1.44 MB disk? _____

11. List three different responsibilities of the floppy disk controller:

    a. _____

    b. _____

    c. _____

12. What type of cable connects the floppy drive to the motherboard?

    _____

13. How many floppy drives can a computer support on a ribbon cable? _____

14. What type of power supply connector supplies power to the floppy drive?

    _____

Worksheet 2.3.14: Hard Drive Identification

1. Explain what a hard drive is used for in a computer:

_____

_____

_____

2. Define the following parts of a hard drive:

   a. Spindle: _____

   _____

   b. Logic Board: _____

   _____

   c. Head Actuator: _____

   _____

   d. Read/Write Heads: _____

   _____

   e. Track: _____

   _____

   f. Sectors: _____

   _____

   g. Disk Platters: _____

   _____

   h. Interface Connector: _____

   _____

   i. Servo Mechanism: _____

   _____

3. In revolutions per minute (rpm), how fast do hard drives spin? _____

4. Flux is the _____ in the media.

5. _____- is an encoding method commonly used on magnetic disks, including RLL, SCSI, IDE, and ESDI.

Worksheet 2.3.15: CD-ROM Identification

1. Explain how a CD-ROM is used: _____

_____

2. Define the following components of a CD-ROM:

a. Laser: _____

_____

b. Pits: _____

_____

c. Lands: _____

_____

d. Servomotor: _____

_____

c. Photo Detector: _____

_____

d. Constant Linear Velocity: _____

_____

e. Constant Angular Velocity: _____

_____

f. Transfer Rate: _____

_____

3. List three common CD-ROM drive speeds found in computers today and identify their transfer rate:

a. _____

b. _____

c. _____

4. What type of power connection is used on a CD-ROM drive? _____

5. What is the audio out cable on a CD-ROM drive connected to in the computer?

_____

6. How much information can be stored on a CD-ROM? _____

7. List two types of interface controllers used by CD-ROM drives:

    a. _____

    b. _____

Lab 3.3.5: The Computer Case and Power Supply

Estimated Time: 45 Minutes

Objective

In this lab, you identify the type of computer case to be used, the form factor of the unit, and the voltage selector switch on the power supply. The inventory of all the components that will be installed in the computer case is discussed. Finally, motherboard standoffs will be installed to prepare the case for the installation of the motherboard.

Equipment

The following equipment is required for this exercise:

- Electrostatic discharge (ESD) wrist strap
- Tool kit and screws
- Computer case with power supply
- Motherboard standoffs and screws
- Motherboard and manual
- Devices that will not be installed yet, but are referenced:
  - o CD-ROM drive, sound card, modem, network interface card (NIC), random-access memory (RAM), hard drive with Integrated Drive Electronics (IDE) cable, floppy drive with cable, mouse, keyboard, monitor

Scenario

You are assembling a personal computer for a friend and are ready to prepare the case for the installation of the motherboard.

Procedures

Wear the antistatic wrist strap during the entire installation process! One end should be looped snugly around the wrist, with the other end attached to an un-painted metallic part of the computer case. This prevents an ESD, which can be extremely hazardous to the computer's sensitive devices.

Step 1

The first step in the assembly process is to create an inventory of all computer components that will be installed into the computer.

Lay out the computer components that will be used in this chapter's labs.

Gather all the information necessary to fill out the following inventory sheet:

Computer Identification	Name: _____ Number: _____
Case	Number of 3.5" bays _____ 5.25" bays _____ Manufacturer: _____
Motherboard	Manufacturer: _____ Model: _____ Bus Speed_____ MHz Form Factor _____AT _____ATX Chipset Manufacturer:_____ Model: _____ BIOS Manufacturer:_____ Version: _____ Does the CPU use a socket or a slot? _____ How many CPU socket/slots are there? _____ How many ISA slots are there? _____ How many PCI slots are there? _____ How many EIDE connectors are there? _____ How many floppy connectors are there? _____ How many serial ports are there? _____ How many parallel ports are there? _____ Is there an AGP slot? _____ How many USB ports are there? _____ How many other ports or slots are there? _____ What kind(s) are they? _____
CPU	Manufacturer: _____ Model: _____ Speed _____ MHz
Memory	_____ 30-pin SIMMs _____ 72-pin SIMMs _____ 168-pin DIMMs _____ 160-pin RIMMs _____ 184-pin RIMMs _____ Others: _____ How many memory slots are there? _____ What is the fastest type of memory supported? _____ What is the maximum memory supported? _____
Hard Drive	Manufacturer: _____ Model: _____ Size: _____ Cylinders: _____ Heads: _____ SPT: _____ Interface Type _____ IDE _____ SCSI

CD-ROM Drive	Manufacturer: _____ Model: _____ Speed: _____ Interface Type _____ IDE _____ SCSI
Floppy Disk Drive	Manufacturer: _____
Monitor	Manufacturer: _____ Model Number: _____
Video Card	Manufacturer: _____ Model: _____ Memory _____ MB ISA _____ PCI _____ On Board_____
Sound Card	Manufacturer: _____ Model: _____ ISA _____ PCI _____ On Board _____
Mouse	Type _____ PS/2 _____ Serial _____ USB
Keyboard	Connector _____ 5-pin DIN or _____ 6-pin mini DIN _____ USB (Make sure it matches the connector on your motherboard.)
Power Supply	AT _____ ATX _____ Other _____ Power Supply Wattage _____

Step 2

Examine the screws that are used for the case. Are the screws Phillips, Flathead, Posidriver, or Torx? _____

Examine the computer case. Is it an AT or ATX case? _____

Briefly describe the difference between an AT and ATX case:

_____

Is the case a desktop, mini-tower, mid-tower, or a full tower? _____

Step 3

Most computer cases come complete with a power supply. Not all cases are built for the U.S. market and therefore might not be set for the correct voltage. Look in the back of the case for the voltage selector switch. If in the United States, make sure that the switch is set to 115 volts. Adhere to the local power requirements when selecting the voltage for the power supply.

Step 4

Power supplies are rated by wattage, which is usually between 250 and 300 watts.

What is the power supply rating for the case? _____

Step 5

Attach the motherboard standoffs to the case. Standoffs are small pegs made of a nonconductive material that help avoid short circuits by preventing the motherboard from touching the case. Look at the holes on the motherboard to help place the standoffs in the proper locations.

Troubleshooting

An equipment list can help solve problems before they start. If there is an item missing, it allows you to find it before the job is half done.

Reflection

Were you able to fill out all areas of the inventory list? _____

Explain any difficulties with the installation:

_____

_____

Lab 3.5.3: Motherboard Installation

Estimated Time: 45 Minutes

Objective

Upon completion of this lab, the motherboard will be placed into the case and secured. The CPU, the heat sink, and the memory will also be installed.

Equipment

The following equipment is required for this exercise:

- ESD wrist strap and antistatic mat
- Tool kit and screws
- Motherboard and manual
- CPU with fan and heat sink
- Thermal grease
- RAM (use the appropriate type for your motherboard)

Scenario

The case for your friend's computer should be ready for the next step. Continue to work on installing the CPU and RAM.

Procedures

You must wear an antistatic wrist strap for this lab, and use extreme care. One discharge of static electricity could render a motherboard useless. In this lab, continue to work on the PC that is being built and properly install the motherboard, CPU, heat sink, CPU fan, and RAM.

Step 1

Lay the motherboard down on the antistatic mat. Identify the CPU socket on the motherboard. The CPU socket is keyed so that the CPU can only be inserted one way.

What CPU type does the motherboard support? _____

Step 2

Pick up the CPU, locating pin one. The CPU can be inserted only one way into the CPU socket.

Install the CPU into the CPU socket. If the CPU is being installed into a zero-insertion-force (ZIF) socket, no force is necessary. If any force needs to be applied, the CPU is not lined up correctly.

After the CPU is seated, adjust the CPU socket lever until it is in the locked position. When the lever is locked, the CPU is secure.

Who is the manufacturer of the CPU? _____

Step 3

Attach the cooling fan to the heat sink. Use the four screws that came with the cooling fan to attach the fan securely to the top of the heat sink.

Note: Some heat sinks are already equipped with a fan and do not need to be secured with screws.

Is the heat sink being installed attached with screws? _____

Step 4

To attach the fan-heat-sink assembly to the CPU, lay the heat sink down on the CPU and align the heat sink clips to their correct positions on the CPU socket. If necessary, rock the heat sink into position until one side of the heat sink is locked down to the outside of the CPU socket. Next, push down the other clip until it locks. After both sides of the heat sink are clipped, the heat sink is secured to the CPU.

Caution: *Using a screwdriver might be necessary to secure the heat sink clips, but do not apply excessive force. If the screwdriver slips off the clips, it might damage the motherboard.*

Step 5

Attach the power connection for the heat sink fan to the motherboard. Use the motherboard manual to identify the fan's power pins on the motherboard. Connect the fan's power leads to these pins and make sure that they are secure and in the correct orientation.

Step 6

Install the memory. When installing the memory, the first step is to identify the memory sockets. Use the motherboard's manual to identify the memory sockets.

Examine the memory sockets and the memory chip(s). Memory and associated sockets are keyed to ensure proper installation. Take the memory and line it up with the socket. Slowly seat the memory into socket one. It might help to rock the memory into the socket until secure by gently pushing alternately on the ends of the chip. Remember, just as with the installation of the CPU, if too much force is exerted, the motherboard can be damaged or destroyed.

If more than one memory chip is to be installed, follow the instructions in the motherboard's manual to add more. It is common for the next memory chip to be placed in socket two. Refer to the motherboard's manual for specific information.

Step 7

Install the motherboard. Align the motherboard with the standoffs and set it in the case. You might have to push the motherboard back slightly against the Input/Output (I/O) plate to get it to line up correctly. After the motherboard is seated, use the proper screws to secure it to the case. Do not over tighten the screws or the board might be damaged.

Step 8

Connect the front panel light emitting diodes (LEDs) to the motherboard. The motherboard connects to the LEDs on the front panel of the computer case to give the operational status of the computer. For example, a green LED on the front panel indicates that the computer is running.

Use the video demonstration or the motherboard's manual to identify all the LED pin outs.

Connect each LED wire to the appropriate pin outs.

Troubleshooting

Proper installation of the cooling fan is absolutely necessary with newer processors. They run at high temperatures and can either cause diminished performance or, in rare cases, be destroyed if not cooled properly.

Reflection

What would happen if the CPU fan stopped during normal computer operations?

_____

_____

What was the most difficult component to install? Why?

_____

_____

Lab 3.6.4: Floppy Drive, Hard Drive, and CD-ROM Installation

Estimated Time: 45 Minutes

Objective

In this lab, you install the floppy drive, hard drive, and CD-ROM drive. Also, you install the ribbon cables for each drive and the audio cable for the CD-ROM drive.

Equipment

The following equipment is required for this exercise:

- The computer case you have been working on
- ESD wrist strap
- Safety glasses
- Tool kit and screws
- Floppy drive with ribbon cable
- Hard drive with ribbon cable
- CD-ROM drive with ribbon cable and audio cable

Scenario

Continue to install the components necessary to complete your friend's computer.

Procedures

When installing devices that use ribbon cables to communicate with the motherboard, such as hard drives and floppy drives, it is important to note the location of pin 1. Examine the ribbon cable and find the red stripe on one side of the cable. Pin 1 is found on the side of the ribbon with the red stripe. The motherboard documentation should show the location of pin 1 for each connector, and pin 1 is also usually labeled on the motherboard for each connector.

Step 1

If the computer case is on its side, move it to the upright position. Locate the half-height (3.5") bays. Locate the top 3.5" bay, if there are two. This is where the floppy drive will be installed. From within the case, reach into the bay and push out the cover for this bay.

Step 2

Retrieve the floppy drive and line it up with the upper 3.5" bay. Slide it in until the front lines up with the front of the computer case and the screw holes on the floppy drive line up with the side rails on the case. Use the proper screws and secure the floppy drive to the case. On some cases, a long screwdriver might be needed to reach the backside of the floppy drive.

Step 3

Install the hard drive. The 3.5" cover for the hard drive bay does not need to be removed. Line up the hard drive with the lower 3.5" bay. Slide the hard drive in until screw holes line up with the case rails. Use the proper screws and secure the hard drive to the case.

Step 4

Install the CD-ROM drive into any of the 5.25" bays. In most computer cases, the 5.25" bays are the upper bays.

Locate the 5.25" bay that you will use for the CD-ROM drive. Reach into the bay and push out the cover for this bay. Retrieve the CD-ROM drive from the parts inventory and slide it in from the front of the case. Push it back until it is flush with the case and the screw holes line up with the case rails. Use the proper screws and secure the CD-ROM drive to the case.

Step 5

The floppy drive is connected to the motherboard with a thirty-four pin, two-connector ribbon cable, which has a twist in it. The twist identifies one of the floppy drives as drive A:\. Only one floppy drive is used during this installation. A second floppy drive can be connected to the second connector on the ribbon cable, and it is assigned as the B:\ drive.

Select the proper ribbon cable for the floppy drive. Take one end of the ribbon cable and connect it to the back of the floppy drive. Take the other end and connect it to the floppy connector on the motherboard. Do not use excessive force when inserting the ribbon cable. Also, make sure the plug is oriented correctly according to pin 1.

Step 6

The CD-ROM drive is attached by using an IDE, forty-pin, forty-conductor ribbon cable. The CD-ROM drive cable has two connectors: one for the motherboard and one for the CD-ROM drive.

Select the proper ribbon cable for the CD-ROM drive. Take one end of the ribbon cable and connect it to the back of the CD-ROM drive. Take the other end and connect it to the IDE connector on the motherboard. Do not bend the motherboard with excessive force when inserting the ribbon cable.

Step 7

Connect the audio cable that came with the CD-ROM drive. Attach one end of the cable to the CD-ROM drive and the other end to the motherboard. Usually, the audio cable connectors are notched and will plug in only one way. If this is not the case, simply insert the connectors whichever way they can go in. The only difference it makes is that the audio channels might be swapped.

If you don't get any sound after the computer is powered up and the CD-ROM drive is tested, simply go back in the box, pull out the audio cable, and reverse the sides. Always consult any manuals that come with components for additional direction on installations.

Step 8

The hard drive is attached by using an IDE, forty-pin, eighty-conductor ribbon cable. The hard drive ribbon cable looks similar to the CD-ROM drive cable. However, for each conductor, it has an associated ground wire, therefore, eighty conductors. This cable can fit into a CD-ROM drive and vice versa, but the hard drive will not work properly if they are switched. The easiest way to tell the difference between the CD-ROM drive ribbon cable and the hard drive cable is to feel them. Because the hard drive cable has eighty conductors, it is not as coarse as the CD-ROM drive cable.

Select the proper ribbon cable for the hard drive. Take one end of the ribbon cable and connect it to the back of the hard drive. Take the other end and connect it to the IDE connector on the motherboard. Do not bend the motherboard when inserting the ribbon cable.

Step 9

The power cables are attached to the motherboard and each drive. Examine the power cables that extend from the power supply. There is one large connector and several smaller connectors. The large 20-pin (ATX 1) attaches to the motherboard, and the smaller connectors attach to the drives.

Most power supplies support four IDE drives and two floppy drives. The connectors for the floppy drives and the IDE drives (CD-ROM drive and hard drive) are different. Examine the back of each drive. Find the power connectors on the back of each drive and connect the correct power cable to each one.

Next, connect the ATX power connector. Use caution when attaching the ATX cable. Do not bend the motherboard.

Troubleshooting

If the floppy ribbon cable is keyed (can plug in only one way), but the floppy drive does not have a keyed slot, check for a punch out on the drive that can be removed to make room for the keyed slot. Otherwise, you need a nonkeyed floppy ribbon cable that can be purchased at a local computer supply store.

Reflection

Briefly summarize the differences between the floppy drive and hard drive ribbon cables:

_____

_____

Write one tip that you learned from the material or in class that helped you with the installation of the components in this lab:

_____

_____

_____

Lab 3.7.1: Video Card Installation and System Booting

Estimated Time: 30 Minutes

Objective

Upon completion of this lab, you will have installed the video card. Also, you will have connected the mouse, keyboard, and monitor. If everything is installed properly, you will be able to turn on the computer at the end of this lab.

Equipment

The following equipment is required for this exercise:

- ESD wrist strap
- Tool kit and screws
- Video card
- PS/2 mouse
- PS/2 keyboard
- 15" monitor
- 3.5" DOS boot floppy
- Motherboard manual

Scenario

Your friend cannot wait any longer for the computer to be finished. It is time to put the finishing touches on the machine and start it up.

Procedure

Before you power up your computer, it is extremely important to properly seat all the expansion cards. If a card is not properly seated when the computer is turned on, it will malfunction. Also, excessive force when seating an expansion card can damage the motherboard, so the job must be done carefully.

Step 1

Recall from Chapter 2 that video cards are built for either the protocol control information (PCI) slot or the Accelerated Graphics Port (AGP) slot. Check the video card that is included in the equipment inventory. In the following space, describe the video card. Include how much video RAM is on the card and whether it is a PCI or an AGP card.

_____

_____

To install the video card, first remove the slot protector from the back of the computer case. Locate the AGP slot or an available PCI slot. Remove the slot protector by removing the screw that holds it in place.

Step 2

Insert the video card into the AGP or PCI slot. If necessary, rock it gently until it is seated on the motherboard. After the video card is seated, line up the hole in the video card bracket with its corresponding hole in the computer case. Use a case screw to secure the video card to the computer case.

Note: Never leave a slot open without a card in it. Leaving a slot open will cause poor air circulation in the case and some components might overheat.

Step 3

Before closing the computer case, review the following checklist:

____ Are there any loose screws in the computer case?

____ Have all tools been removed from the computer case?

____ Is the voltage selector switch in the correct position?

____ Is the CPU seated completely?

____ Is the fan secured?

____ Is the fan plugged in?

____ Is the memory in the correct slot, and is it fully seated?

____ Are all the drives in their correct position and secure to the chassis?

____ Are the ribbon cables fully seated and connected to the correct drives?

____ Is the audio cable connected to the CD-ROM drive correctly?

____ Is the ATX 1 power cable in the right position and has it been latched down?

After completing the checklist, put the computer case together. Attach all the case panels and secure them with the appropriate screws.

Step 4

Locate the two PS/2 ports on the back of the computer. One port is designated for the mouse and the other for the keyboard. Look closely at these ports. On newer motherboards, there is an icon for the mouse and keyboard. Also, each port might be color-coded: purple for the keyboard and green for the mouse. Plug the mouse and keyboard into their respective ports by lining up the pins and pinholes and pushing on the connections. Do not push too hard, but make sure they are inserted all the way.

Step 5

Locate the monitor and place it within about one foot of the computer. Examine the video card adapter that was installed in Step 1. It will be a 15-pin female connector. Examine the monitor connector. It will be a 15-pin male connector. Line up the pins to the pinholes and connect the monitor cable to the video adaptor. Most cables come with monitor screws already attached. Tighten these screws evenly until the monitor cable is attached to the video card.

Step 6

Now plug in the computer's power cable. On ATX models, a power switch will be on the back of the computer and a power button will be on the front. Turn on the power switch first. The computer will not power up because both the switch and the button must be on.

Now, push the power button on the front panel of the computer. This powers up the computer. Some front panel LEDs will turn on, and you will hear the power supply fan spin up.

Step 7

Press the appropriate key to cause the computer to go into the Basic Input/Output System (BIOS) setup mode. (Some BIOS manufacturers use a different key, or key combination, to enter BIOS configuration mode. When you first power up the computer, a message displays something similar to "Press F3 to enter Setup.") If this message does not display, consult your motherboard's manual for the correct button or sequence of keys.

When the computer goes into BIOS setup, the main menu screen displays. Run through the BIOS settings below and boot the computer from a bootable floppy disk.

Move around the screen by using the arrow keys until the Standard Complementary Metal Oxide Semiconductor (CMOS) menu item is highlighted.

Press the **Enter** key to open the Standard CMOS features screen. On this screen, you can change the time, date, and the type of drives this computer will recognize.

Check to see if the BIOS recognizes Drive A. Does it show Drive A as a 1.44 MB, 3.5" floppy? _____

Check to see if there is a Drive B. Because a second floppy drive was not connected when the system was built, you should not find one.

To leave the BIOS setup, press the **Esc** key. A prompt displays that asks if you want to quit without saving; press the **Y** key for yes.

Step 8

In this step, the computer is booted from a floppy disk. Restart the computer and insert the 3.5" bootable floppy disk. If the standard BIOS settings have not been altered, the computer will look for the operating system in the following order: 1) removable media, 2) hard drive, and 3) CD-ROM drive. During normal operations, the computer is booted without a floppy disk; therefore, the computer skips the floppy and finds the operating system on the hard drive.

Recall from Chapter 2 that DOS is a command line operating system. After the computer boots, the screen displays an A:\> prompt; there will not be any windows or icons.

Use the DOS boot disk to check some basic functions of the computer. Run the following DOS command and write out the results:

Type **dir** and press **Enter**.

What are the results of typing this command?

_____

_____

_____

_____

Troubleshooting

Did the computer boot correctly? _____

If not, go over the checklist again. Have the instructor or lab aide look over the system.

How many beeps did you hear? _____

If the computer did not boot correctly, what steps did you take to troubleshoot it?

_____

_____

Reflection

Did everything go as expected? If not, why not?

_____

_____

What would have made the construction of the computer easier? Describe a tip or technique that you learned when building this computer that you would use in the future.

_____

_____

_____

Worksheet 3.3.4: Power Supplies

1. Depending on the type of case and motherboard selected, the power supply must adhere to the same _____ requirements to fit inside the case and correctly power the motherboard and other devices.

2. Some fans can change direction to allow air to be blown directly on the _____ and to regulate the quality of the air entering the case.

3. The two basic types of power supplies are the following:

    a._____

    b._____

4. Match each component with the voltage from the power supply unit that it uses:

    1. ____ Motherboard   a. −5V

    2. ____ Disk drives   b. +3.3V

    3. ____ Serial port circuits   c. 0V

    4. ____ ISA bus cards   d. +12V

    5. ____ Most newer CPUs   e. +5V

    6. ____ Ground   f. −12V

5. An AT power supply produces how many different levels of DC voltage? _____

6. An ATX power supply produces how many different levels of DC voltage? _____

7. Match each voltage with the correct color wire:

    1. ____ Yellow   a. 0V

    2. ____ Red   b. −5V

    3. ____ Blue   c. +3.3V

    4. ____ White   d. +12V

    5. ____ Black   e. +5V

    6. ____ Orange   f. −12V

8. Never attempt to repair a defective power supply. _____inside a power supply box stores electricity and discharges through the body if touched.

9. The ATX motherboard is a _____-pin keyed connector.

10. The AT motherboard has two _____-pin connectors.

11. The ATX motherboard directs air _____ of the computer case.

12. The AT motherboard directs air _____ of the computer case.

Worksheet 3.9.1: What is BIOS?

1. The acronym BIOS stands for _____.

2. The BIOS code is typically embedded in a _____ chip on the motherboard.

3. _____ BIOS allows the upgrade of the BIOS software from a disk provided by the manufacturer without replacing the chip.

4. Configuration of the BIOS on a computer is called the _____ or _____.

5. Without the correct code and _____, the system will either not boot properly or work inconsistently with frequent errors.

6. The acronym POST stands for _____.

7. Any problems during the POST are indicated by the BIOS displaying _____.

8. BIOS initially runs basic device test programs and then seeks to _____ these devices.

9. Circle all that are correct:

    1. BIOS contains the software required to test hardware at bootup.
    2. BIOS contains the software required to execute windows applications and access user files.
    3. BIOS contains the software required to support the transfer of data between hardware components.
    4. BIOS contains the software required to support hard drive and floppy drive data storage.
    5. BIOS contains the software required to start up the operating system.

10. BIOS is saved in the chip on the motherboard (even when the power is turned off) by a _____.

Lab 4.2.3: Basic DOS Commands

Estimated Time: 30 Minutes

Objective

Upon completion of this lab, you will be able to navigate the DOS command line. You will also be able to perform basic file management tasks that include the following: creating directories and files, navigating through directories, displaying the content of directories, and displaying and changing file attributes.

Equipment

The following equipment is required for this exercise:

- Computer with a version of DOS running

Scenario

Your manager asked you to create a directory structure using the DOS command line. She wants you to create a directory in which documents for the upcoming inventory will be kept. The directory structure your manager wants you to create is C:\IT\pcs. She has also asked you to create a read-only test file.

Procedures

The following steps detail the process of managing files by using the DOS command line. Basic DOS commands will carry out the task presented by your manager. At the end, the newly created directories and test file you have created will be deleted safely.

Step 1

You can access the DOS prompt (command line) a few different ways. The most common way is to boot into a version of Windows, press **Start Menu** > **Run**, >and type **command**. You can also access it by pressing **Start Menu** > **Programs** > **Accessories** > and selecting **Command Prompt**. If Windows won't load, you can access the DOS prompt by pressing **F8** during the boot process and selecting **Safe mode with command prompt**.

As shown in Figure 1, when DOS is accessed, the window displays the C prompt (C:\>).

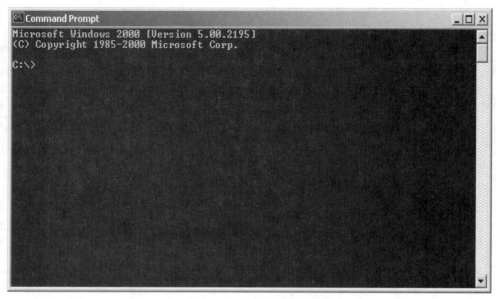

Figure 1 — DOS Prompt

Step 2

At the C prompt, type **dir** to show a list of the directories located on this drive.

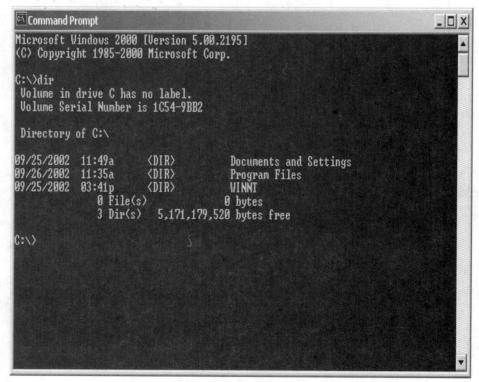

Figure 2 — Using the DIR Command

Figure 2 shows the DIR command lists directories and various files. Directories are specified with the <DIR> notation that precedes the file/directory. The DIR command also displays the volume name, free space, and total files and directories present.

Step 3

To create directories in DOS, use the **md** *directory_name* or *mkdir directory_name* command. Type **md IT** to create the IT directory.

```
C:\>md IT
```

Step 4

Next, display the IT directory by using the **dir** command at the root (C:\>). Figure 3 shows the newly created IT directory.

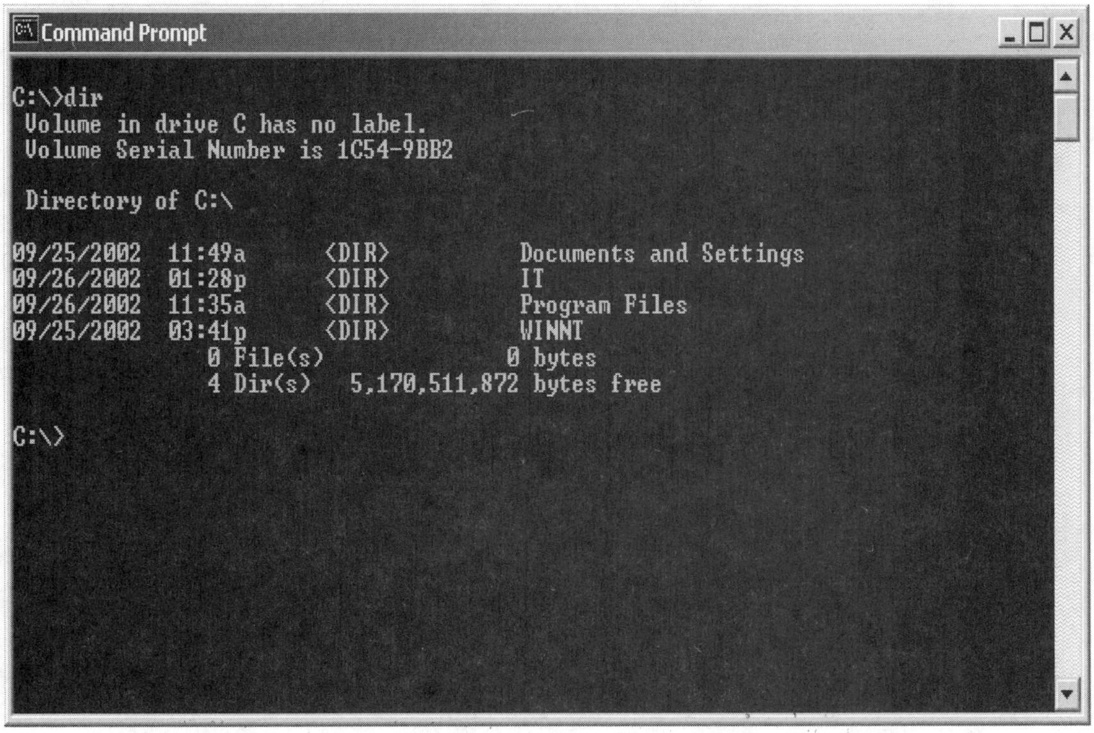

Figure 3 — Creating a Directory in DOS

Step 5

To change directories, use the **cd** *directory_name* or **chdir** *directory_name* command. For example, to access the IT directory, type **C:\>cd IT**. Typing this command changes the C prompt to C:\IT>.

Step 6

The command prompt should now be C:\IT>. The next task is to create another directory called pcs.

What command makes this directory?

_____

Step 7

Navigate to the newly created pcs directory.

What command changes to the pcs directory?

_____

What does the command line look like?

_____

Step 8

To create a file in DOS, use the **copy con** *filename* command. This command copies a file from the console (con) and places it in your directory. The console in this case is your screen. After you type this command, you will have a blank line on the command prompt. You can then type in text that will be saved in the newly created file. When you are finished typing in your message, hold down the Control Key (<**Ctrl**>) press the **Z** key, and press the **Enter** key. This key combination ends the message and DOS displays *1 file(s) copied*.

```
C:\IT\pcs>copy con sample.txt
This is an inventory test document
<Ctrl>+Z
<Enter>
1 file(s) copied
```

Step 9

Display the contents of the pcs directory. The newly created sample.txt in your directory is displayed. Figure 4 shows the DOS output for the DIR command in the pcs directory.

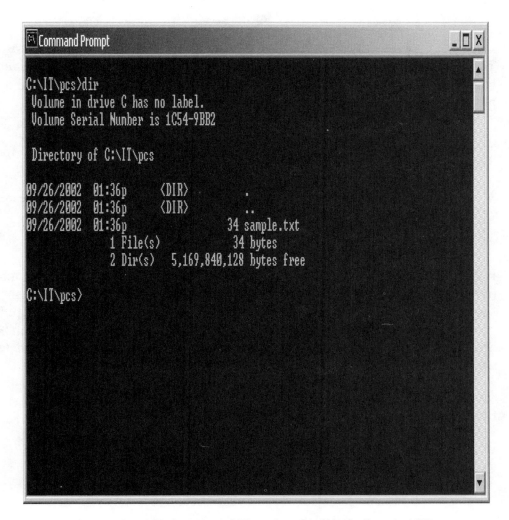

Figure 4 — DIR Command Showing the Newly Created File

Step 10

Next, display the attributes for the sample.txt file. To display the attributes of a file, type **attrib** *filename.* Valid attribute values are as follows:

- R – Read-only file attribute

- A – Archive file attribute

- S – System file attribute

- H – Hidden file attribute

What command would you type to display the attributes of sample.txt?

_____

What are the attributes of sample.txt?

_____

Step 11

To change or remove an attribute, use the **attrib [-/+]** *attribute_value filename* command. The minus (-) option removes an attribute value from a file, and the plus (+) option adds an attribute value to a file. As discussed earlier, valid attribute values are R (read-only), A (archive), S (system), and H (hidden).

What command changes the attribute value of the sample.txt file to a read-only file?

_____

Troubleshooting

If a command is unclear or forgotten, DOS provides useful command information. DOS provides general command syntax or detailed information about a specific command. The command to list all available commands is c:\>**help**. This command can be used at any level within the DOS structure. To find specific information about a command, including proper syntax and optional parameters, use the c:\>*command* **/?** command.

Reflection

What is the command to make a directory?

_____

What is the command to delete or remove a directory?

_____

List the four different attributes that a file can be assigned?

_____

_____

Lab 4.2.4: Creating a DOS Boot Disk

Estimated Time: 25 Minutes

Objective

Upon completion of this lab, you will know which files are necessary to make a floppy disk bootable. Also, you will know the commands necessary to create a boot disk.

Equipment

The following equipment is required for this exercise:

- Operational computer with Windows 98 or below installed
- Blank floppy diskette

Note: This lab will not work with Windows ME, Windows 2000, or Windows XP.

Scenario

As a computer technician, you need to create a boot disk to prepare a computer for installation. This disk must include utilities such as fdisk and format so that a hard drive can be prepared for an operating system.

Procedures

Formatting prepares the disk for use. For DOS, make a bootable disk by using the same version of DOS that is on your hard drive.

Use caution so that you do not accidentally format the hard drive.

Step 1

If the computer is not already booted and at a DOS prompt, turn it on now. Put a floppy diskette into the drive and format the floppy diskette by using the following command: C:\>**FORMAT A: /S**

Which three files are necessary to make the disk bootable?

_____ , _____ , _____

Step 2

Leave the diskette in the drive and reboot the system. This process tests the disk to make sure that it is bootable.

Did the system successfully boot to a prompt? _____

What does the prompt look like? _____

Step 3

When the system boots using Microsoft's DOS, five files are involved: autoexec.bat, command.com, config.sys, io.sys, and msdos.sys.

Assuming that all five files are available on a bootable disk, in what order are these files accessed when the system is booted?

1. _____

2. _____

3. _____

4. _____

5. _____

Step 4

In addition to the five files just mentioned, certain utilities can be helpful when working with a computer that does not have an operating system:

- DEFRAG.EXE
- EDIT.COM (which might also require QBASIC.EXE if you are using an older version of DOS)
- FDISK.EXE
- FORMAT.COM
- MEM.EXE
- SCANDISK.EXE
- SYS.COM
- UNDELETE.EXE

Troubleshooting

Often, a computer is restarted without removing the floppy disk from the floppy drive. If the disk is not bootable (does not have io.sys, msdos.sys, and command.com), an error message that says *Non-System disk or disk error. Replace and strike any key when ready* displays. It is possible that you did not use the /S switch if you get this message after formatting a disk. Double check that the disk has the proper files on it to make it bootable.

Reflection

List any other utilities that are useful on a boot disk:

_____

_____

Worksheet 4.1.3: Operating System Fundamentals

Answer the following true or false questions:

1. _____ Two or more users running programs and sharing peripheral devices, such as a printer, at the same time is known as multitasking.

2. _____ Multitasking is a computer's capability to run multiple applications at the same time.

3. _____ When a computer has two or more central processing units (CPUs) that programs share, it is known as multiprocessing.

4. _____ Multithreading is not the capability of a program to be broken into smaller parts so that it can be loaded as needed by the operating system.

5. _____ Multithreading allows individual programs to be multitasked.

6. _____ UNIX has been around since the 1960s.

7. _____ Computers that are not capable of handling concurrent users and multiple jobs are often called network servers or servers.

8. _____ The file management system is what the OS uses to organize and manage files.

Worksheet 4.2.7: DOS

True or False:

1. _____ DOS is an acronym for Data Operating Service.

2. _____ All generations of Windows to date support DOS commands.

3. _____ DOS is user friendly.

4. _____ DOS can only run a single program at a time.

5. _____ DOS can run large programs.

6. _____ DOS is an essential tool used extensively for troubleshooting.

7. _____ DOS files on a disk are stored in folders.

8. _____ DOS records the location of every directory and file on a disk in a table called the FAT.

9. _____ DOS files are referred to as filenames that comprise up to eight characters and an extension.

10. _____ DOS filenames and their extensions are separated by a dash (-).

11. _____ DOS has a main directory on the disk known as the tree directory.

12. _____ The root of the C drive is represented by "C:\".

13. _____ The directory name and filename are separated by a slash (/).

Worksheet 4.2.3: DOS Commands

Match each command with the function it performs:

1. ____DIR		a. Copies a file
2. ____CD		b. Displays memory properties
3. ____MD		c. Displays the status of a disk
4. ____RD		d. Changes the attributes of a file
5. ____DEL		e. Copies one floppy disk to another
6. ____REN		f. Formats a disk
7. ____SET		g. Displays the contents of a directory
8. ____MEM		h. Sets the system time
9. ____COPY		i. Prints a text document
10. ____TYPE		j. Opens a file for editing
11. ____FDISK		k. Removes a directory
12. ____TIME		l. Deletes a file
13. ____DATE		m. Creates a new directory
14. ____CHKDSK		n. Renames a file
15. ____DISKCOPY		o. Displays the contents of the environment variables
16. ____EDIT		p. Changes to a specified directory
17. ____FORMAT		q. Program that formats and partitions fixed disks
18. ____PRINT		r. Displays the contents of a text file
19. ____ATTRIB		s. Sets the system date

Lab 5.1.6: Changing File Views in Windows (Showing File Extensions)

Estimated Time: 20 Minutes

Objective

Upon completion of this lab, you will be able to change the file view based on your needs or preferences.

Equipment

The following equipment is required for this exercise:

- Computer running Windows 9x

Scenario

While navigating through your folders, you realize that the files and subfolders could be arranged better. You feel the default display is not the best visual display for your files. In this lab, you change the File View to your personal preferences.

Procedures

Changing the file view in Windows can reveal important information about files and subfolders. Users can find information on file size, file type, and time and date of the last modification. Also, the view can be configured based on personal preferences. View preferences include thumbnails, list, or large or small icons. Configuring the file view is especially helpful when a folder contains numerous files or subfolders. Folder contents can be neatly displayed according to preference or needs, which simplifies navigation.

Step 1

Start the computer into the Windows Desktop environment.

Step 2

Next, double-click the **My Computer** icon on the Desktop to open the window. My Computer is accessed through the Start menu in Windows XP.

Step 3

While the cursor is pointed at a blank space in the My Computer window, right-click and select the **View** option. Figure 1 displays the right-click menu.

Figure 1 — Selecting the View Option

When selecting the View option, what parameters are available?

_____

_____

Step 4

Next, select the **View** parameter for the files. Notice how icons in the folder change.

What information is displayed when the Details option is selected?

_____

_____

Step 5

After selecting the **View** option, set this view for all folders. To do this, select **Tools** > **Folder Options**. Figure 2 shows this process.

Figure 2 — Selecting the Folder Options

After you select **Folder Options** from the **Tool** menu, the Folder Options display box appears. Figure 3 shows the Folder Options display box.

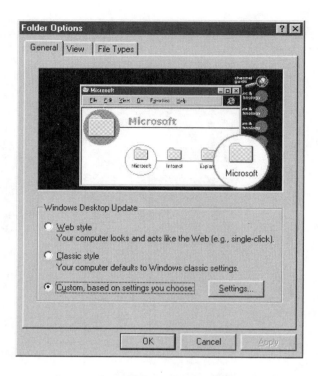

Figure 3 — Folder Options Display Box

Step 6

Next, select the **View** tab. What options are available in the View tab?

_____

_____

Step 7

From the View tab, select the **Like Current Folder** command button. Selecting this button makes the view in the current folder universal throughout the drive.

Figure 4 — Folder Options Display Box

Troubleshooting

Changing your file view customizes the preferences. Also, important details and system files can be viewed by using advanced options in the Folder Options window. System files are usually hidden to protect against accidental deletion, but there are times when it is necessary to configure these files.

Reflection

How can files in a folder be rearranged?

_____

_____

Why would a user want to change their folder view settings?

_____

_____

Lab 5.1.7: Text Editing and File Management

Estimated Time: 30 Minutes

Objective

Upon completion of this lab, you will be introduced to creating a file in Notepad, saving it to your hard drive, creating a folder on a floppy disk, and moving the file from the hard drive to the floppy disk.

Equipment

The following equipment is required for this exercise:

- Lab computer with Windows 9x installed

- 3 ½" floppy disk

Scenario

You need to edit a text file for testing a floppy drive that you installed. To do this, you need to create a file, edit it, and move it from one location to another.

Procedures

The creation and management of files in any operating system (OS) is most of what the end user does while on a computer. Whether it is to update, rename, move, or delete a file, knowing how to do all these without thinking twice saves time and effort.

Step 1

From the Windows Desktop, click the **Start** button and move the cursor to **Programs** > **Accessories** > and click **Notepad**.

Step 2

After Notepad is open and on the Desktop, begin typing a message of your choice within the editing area. Type just a few sentences and click the **File** menu and select **Save As....** This opens a new window, which allows you to choose the location of your text file.

The default location is My Documents. If the My Documents folder is not the default, use the **Save In** drop-down box to choose **My Documents**. With My Documents as your folder, type **testfile.txt** within the File name text box and click the **Save** button.

Step 3

The file is now saved on the computer. Notepad can be closed without losing any data.

To manage files on the computer, open a file manager application, such as Windows Explorer. This is found in the Programs menu by clicking the **Start** button and selecting **Programs** and **Windows Explorer**.

Note: An alternate way to open Windows Explorer is to right-click the **Start** button and choose **Explore**.

Step 4

With Windows Explorer open, use the left windowpane to locate the My Documents folder where the text file testfile.txt is saved.

Locate the My Documents folder and click it to display the contents on the right windowpane. As with most things in Windows, there is more than one way to rename a file. You learn both in this step.

The first way to rename a file is to select the file by clicking it once. Then, with the file testfile.txt selected, go to the **File** menu of Windows Explorer and select **Rename**. This outlines the filename with a box and highlights the name of the file. Now type a new filename for the file, such as newname.txt. After the file is renamed, press the **Enter** key to finish the changes.

The other way to rename a file in Windows is to right-click the filename itself and select **Rename** from the drop-down menu. Use this method to rename the file back to the original name testfile.txt.

Both methods work the same; it is merely personal preference as to which way is used.

Step 5

Now, insert a formatted floppy disk into the floppy drive. Navigate Windows Explorer to the 3 ½" floppy drive icon in the left windowpane. When selected, the contents of the floppy disk display in the right windowpane. Create a new folder on the floppy disk; there are two ways to do this.

The first way is to go to the **File** menu, select **New.** Then in the submenu that appears, click **Folder**. This creates an empty folder that needs to be named. In the same way you renamed the text file, give the folder a name such as my test folder and press **Enter** to complete the process.

The second way to create a folder is to right-click in the right windowpane and select **New** and select **Folder**.

Step 6

To move a file from one location to another is a simple process. As always, there is more than one way of doing this. One straightforward method and some short cuts will be discussed.

To move the text file that you created earlier to the folder that was created on the floppy disk, navigate Windows Explorer to the My Documents folder on the computer. From there, select the testfile.txt and go to the **Edit** menu and select **Cut**.

Now navigate Windows Explorer to the folder that you created on the 3 ½" floppy. Highlight the folder that was created, go to the **Edit** menu and select **Paste**.

The file created will be moved from the My Documents folder to the floppy disk. To verify that it worked, navigate Windows Explorer back to the My Documents folder to make sure that the file is not there anymore. Then, navigate back to the floppy and make sure that document testfile.txt appears on the floppy.

Troubleshooting

Knowing how to cut, copy, and paste quickly saves a lot of time when working within Windows. There are shortcuts to many of the commands within Windows. To cut a file without clicking the Edit menu or right-clicking, simply select a file and type the key combination **Ctrl-X**. Holding the control key and pressing X when a file is selected is the same as selecting Cut from the Edit menu.

Try this with all the shortcut commands.

Reflection

List a method to copy or move files from one location to another by using the mouse only:

_____

_____

Lab 5.4.2: Hard Drive Preparation Using FDISK and FORMAT

Estimated Time: 30 Minutes

Objective

Upon completion of this lab, you will be able to partition the hard drive into two drives. You will also be able to install the three system files onto the hard drive to make it a bootable drive.

Note: This procedure erases any current information on the lab computer's hard drive. Before proceeding, make sure to use only components that can be erased and copied to.

Equipment

The following equipment is required for this exercise:

- Lab computer
- Bootable floppy disk with DOS FDISK and FORMAT commands

Scenario

You have installed a new hard drive in your computer and need to prepare it for an operating system. To do this, you need to use the DOS FDISK and FORMAT commands.

Procedures

After having the hard drive installed into a computer, the drive must be prepared for the computer to communicate with it during the boot process. Using the DOS commands **FDISK** and **FORMAT**, the hard drive can be partitioned and prepared for communication and usage.

Step 1

Boot up the computer using a bootable floppy disk with the **FDISK** and **FORMAT** commands on it.

Step 2

To create and remove partitions, first start the FDISK program. Type **FDISK** at the prompt and press **Enter**. After the application starts, enable large disk support [**y**].

Now, select the partition type to delete from the menu that displays: Primary DOS partition, Extended DOS partition, Logical DOS drives in the Extended partition, or a Non-DOS partition.

If logical drives are defined in the extended partition, they need to be removed before the Extended partition is removed. To delete any partition, simply select the option that correlates with the partition to be removed and follow the directions on the screen.

Step 3

After all the partitions have been removed from the drive, return to the main menu and select **Option 1** to create a DOS partition. Then, from the next menu, select **Option 1** to create a Primary DOS partition. From there, follow the on-screen directions to finish creating the Primary DOS partition.

At this point, exit FDISK and restart the computer with the floppy disk still in the drive.

Note: Make sure to set the Primary Drive to **Active**.

Step 4

After the computer has restarted, it is time to format the partition that was just created. To do this, type **format C: /s** from the command prompt. This tells the format program to make the C drive usable for DOS and the /s copies system files to the hard drive after it is formatted so that it is bootable.

The program gives the option of formatting the drive. This erases anything that is on the drive. Because the drive is empty, type **Y** and press **Enter** to continue.

Step 5

When the format is complete, enter your name when asked to enter a volume label. When the format is complete and the command prompt is returned, restart the computer without the bootable floppy inserted to make sure that the computer will boot from the hard drive.

Troubleshooting

Sometimes, a third-party formatting application is necessary when dealing with certain partition types. If a hard drive does not let you remove a partition, consider purchasing a third-party product, such as Power Quest's Partition Magic, which is available in most computer software stores.

Reflection

List the three files required for booting a DOS formatted disk:

_____ , _____ , _____

What other DOS commands will transfer these system files from one drive to another?

_____

Lab 5.5.5: Windows OS Installation

Estimated Time: 60 Minutes

Objective

Upon completion of this lab, you will be able to install Windows 98.

Equipment

The following equipment is required for this exercise:

- Computer with a partitioned and formatted hard drive
- Bootable floppy disk with CD-ROM drivers or a bootable CD-ROM drive
- Windows 98 Second Edition Install CD

Scenario

You have a friend that has a computer, but he is not sure how to install an operating system. Luckily, you have a deeper knowledge of computers than your friend does and have offered to help him out.

Procedures

For a computer to be useful, it needs an operating system. The most commonly used operating system is Microsoft Windows. This exercise takes approximately an hour to complete. Follow the steps below to install Windows 98.

Note: The same procedures can install other versions of Windows; however, there might be some significant differences during the setup process.

Step 1

Depending on whether the computer supports bootable CDs, you need to insert a bootable floppy disk with CD-ROM support to start. If the computer supports bootable CDs, simply insert the Windows 98 Installation CD and boot the computer. If you see a message on the screen to press a key to boot from the CD, press a key to start.

Step 2

If you are in a situation in which you need to boot from a floppy disk, insert the disk and turn your computer on. After the computer has booted, there should be a DOS prompt that looks like this: A:\>. To begin the installation, change the directory to your CD-ROM drive by typing **D:** and pressing **Enter**. Type **setup** and press **Enter** to begin the installation.

Note: The CD-ROM drive letter might be different in your computer; make any necessary adjustments.

Step 3

The Microsoft Windows 98 Setup screen displays a few different options:

- To set up Windows now, press Enter.
- To learn more about Setup before continuing, press **F1**.
- To quit Setup without installing Windows, press **F3**.
- Press **Enter** to install Windows 98.

Step 4

Prior to the installation, Windows Setup needs to run Scandisk to make sure that there aren't any problems with the hard drive. Press **Enter** to continue and wait for the graphical setup interface to display.

After the Windows 98 Setup screen displays, most of the installation is automated. However, the following steps walk you through the areas that require information to be gathered.

Step 5

After Windows Setup runs Scandisk, you are presented with a series of prompts that lead you through the installation process. When the Windows 98 Setup Wizard displays, you need to select the directory where you want to install Windows 98. Select the checkbox that says **C:\WINDOWS**.

Windows then prepares this directory.

Step 6

Next, a series of Setup Options will be prompted for the installation of Windows 98.

What are the available options available for installing Windows 98?

_____

_____

_____

_____

For the purpose of this lab, select **Typical** and press **Next**.

Step 7

Windows then prompts you with options for installing system components. Select the check box to install the most common components and press **Next**.

Step 8

Setup then gives you the option to identify your computer.

What parameters can be defined to identify your computer?

_____

_____

You can either leave the default computer identification or enter your own information.

Step 9

The Windows 98 Setup Wizard then asks for your location. Make the appropriate selection and continue.

Step 10

Setup then prompts you to *Start Copying Files*. Press **Next** to continue.

Step 11

At this point, a bar graph appears and begins to count up to 100 percent. Speed varies with system hardware. Carefully read the software license. Select **Yes** to agree with the license. Windows Setup then prompts for the CD-KEY. This information is with the Certificate of Authenticity on the CD case.

Enter the key exactly and click **Next** to continue. Click **Finish** to start using Windows 98.

Step 12

Windows runs through a series of automatic hardware detection features. This process of detecting hardware usually takes a few minutes. When Windows finishes detecting your hardware, select date and time properties. Continue through the setup and when prompted, reboot the machine.

Step 13

This should successfully complete the installation of Windows 98.

Troubleshooting

It is possible for Windows Setup to not finish the installation properly. If for some reason there is a problem, run setup again. Additional help and resources are available on Microsoft's web site at www.microsoft.com.

Reflection

Did the Windows installation complete successfully? _____

If you needed to install Windows on another system, do you feel confident that you would be able to? _____

Make note of any tips or tricks you might have learned during the installation.

_____

_____

_____

_____

_____

Lab 5.6.1: Troubleshooting 101

Estimated Time: 20 Minutes

Objective

Upon completion of this lab, you will have learned some basic troubleshooting skills.

Equipment

This lab requires something to write with, a pen or pencil.

Scenario

To be prepared for a situation in which an end user needs help to solve a problem, answer the following questions.

Procedures

Troubleshooting is an important part of a technician's job. Troubleshooting must be approached in a systematic way. One way to do this is by looking at the most obvious things first. Overlooking the obvious can cost time and money. Remember that every time a technician goes into the computer, there is a risk of damaging the computer.

Step 1

Write down the steps a technician should take if a printer is not printing. Put them in order, starting with what a technician should check first.

_____

_____

_____

_____

_____

Step 2

Write down the steps a technician should take if a file cannot be saved onto a floppy disk. Put them in order, starting with what a technician should check first.

_____

_____

_____

_____

_____

Step 3

Write down the steps a technician should take if a monitor is not displaying anything. Put them in order, starting with what a technician should check first.

_____

_____

_____

_____

_____

Step 4

Write down the steps a technician should take if the computer will not turn on. Put them in order, starting with what a technician should check first.

_____

_____

_____

_____

_____

Troubleshooting

When approaching a computer that is reportedly broken, try to rule out the obvious first. Make sure the unit is turned on and that all components are plugged in properly. Also, it can help to ask the user of the system what was the last thing they were doing on the computer before it failed.

Reflection

Troubleshooting requires a systematic approach to solve problems. Choose a problem that is not computer-related, such as the toaster doesn't toast bread. List the steps to take to solve this problem. Is a systematic approach useful in solving noncomputer related problems?

_____

_____

_____

_____

_____

_____

_____

_____

_____

_____

_____

_____

_____

_____

_____

_____

_____

Lab 5.6.4: Installing a Driver

Estimated Time: 20 Minutes

Objective

Upon completion of this lab, you will be able to install the driver for a rollerball mouse. The same process is used when installing any new device on your system.

Equipment

The following equipment is required for this exercise:

- Lab computer with Windows 9x operating system
- Rollerball mouse with the driver disk

Scenario

You have purchased a new rollerball mouse and want to install it.

Procedures

Make sure that you have the proper drivers for the operating system that you have installed. Drivers built for Windows 95 might install properly on a Windows 98 platform but could cause undesirable results.

Step 1

From the Windows 9x Desktop, go to **Start** > **Settings** > **Control Panel**.

Step 2

On the Control Panel, double-click the **Add New Hardware** icon. This starts the Add New Hardware Wizard. Read the onscreen display and click the **Next** button to continue.

Step 3

The Hardware Wizard searches for Plug and Play devices. Click the **Next** button to continue. When the search is complete, the wizard asks if it can search for devices that are not Plug and Play-compatible. Select **No, I want to select the hardware from a list** and click **Next**.

Step 4

A list of hardware devices to choose from displays. Select the device that most closely matches the device being installed, which in this exercise is a **Mouse**. After the device is selected, click **Next**.

Step 5

If the latest driver is on a CD-ROM or floppy disk, insert it into the computer. Click the **Have Disk** button and then either type the path to the driver or click the **Browse** button to find the exact location of the driver. After the driver is selected, click the **OK** button to continue.

At this time, the wizard displays a list consisting of any number of devices, which should match the device being installed. Select the one that matches the device the most and click **Next**.

Step 6

Follow the rest of the on-screen instructions to complete the installation process. When the driver is installed, Windows needs to be restarted for the changes to take effect. If a dialogue box displays to restart, click **Yes**; otherwise, click the **Start** button, select the **Shut Down** option, and shut down the computer.

Step 7

After the computer has been shut off, remove the current mouse and plug the rollerball mouse into the now available PS/2 port. When it has been plugged in properly, turn on the computer. At the Windows Desktop, test the new device. If the device does not respond, see the troubleshooting section of this lab.

Troubleshooting

It is important to use the correct driver when installing a device. For example, a new sound card will most likely not work or will work improperly if the wrong drivers are installed.

Also, using the latest driver is a good practice to follow. When installing a new device, check the manufacturer's web site for the latest drivers available for its product.

If there are problems with the mouse pointer, verify that it is properly connected and that the mouse pointer is clean and free of any dust or debris. If the problem still exists after verifying the connection and cleaning, try restarting the machine. Essentially, rebooting the machine refreshes and reloads the mouse pointer drivers. This should resolve most problems associated with the mouse pointer devices. However, if the problem still exists, the driver might need to be updated. To update the driver, simply repeat the steps outlined in this lab with the latest driver that can usually be found on the Internet.

Reflection

Did you have any problems installing the drivers for this device? _____

If so, explain how the problem was solved:

_____

_____

_____

_____

_____

_____

_____

_____

_____

_____

_____

Lab 5.6.5: Windows Startup Disk

Estimated Time: 15 Minutes

Objective

Upon completion of this exercise, you will be able to create a Windows 9x startup disk.

Equipment

The following equipment is required for this exercise:

- Computer with Windows 9x operating system installed
- One 3 ½" blank disk

Scenario

You have installed the Windows 9x operating system but did not make a Windows startup disk during the installation.

Procedures

After the operating system is up and running, create a Windows 9x startup disk. If for some reason Windows does not load, the boot disk might be necessary to begin the troubleshooting process.

Note: In this lab, use the built-in functionality of Windows 9x to create a Windows startup disk. A boot disk can be made by copying the necessary startup files to a floppy disk.

Step 1

From the Windows 9x Desktop, go to **Start** > **Settings** > **Control Panel**.

What is the general purpose of the Control Panel?

_____

_____

_____

Step 2

After the Control Panel displays, double-click the **Add/Remove Programs** icon. In the Add/Remove Programs Properties window, select the **Startup Disk** tab.

Step 3

Click the **Create Disk** button. A status bar displays indicating that it is preparing the files needed for the startup disk. If the cab files are not available, Windows prompts for the Windows 9x Installation CD.

Step 4

When the files for the startup disk have been collected, Windows prompts you to label a disk and insert it into the drive. Click the **OK** button.

Step 5

After the startup disk has been created, write-protect the disk by moving the switch to the open position. (The switch is located on the back of the disk on the top-left corner.)

Why is it important to write-protect a bootable floppy disk?

_____

_____

Step 6

To finish the process, reboot the system to make sure that the disk works.

Troubleshooting

If you work on computers often, you will most likely have a situation in which you need a bootable floppy disk. If the operating system does not start, a floppy disk can be used to view the contents of the hard drive and begin the troubleshooting.

Reflection

What three files are needed for a floppy disk to boot properly?

_____

_____

_____

Worksheet 5.1.10: Windows Files and Folders

1. A _____ and a _____ are equivalent terms for the same concept—a place to store files.

2. The _____ directory is the master folder that contains all the other folders.

3. Names of early Windows 3.1 and DOS filenames are limited to_____ letters plus a _____ letter extension, but Windows 98 and later allow extended filenames of up to _____ characters.

4. Drive letters use the 26 letters of the alphabet followed by a colon. _____ and _____ are reserved for floppy drives; _____ for the hard drive.

5. By _____-clicking an item on the Desktop or in Explorer, options appear, such as Copy, Move, or Create Shortcuts.

6. _____ give immediate clues as to the creation or last modified date of a file or folder, type of item, and size of the file.

7. To highlight several files at one time, hold down the _____ key and click those files you want to select.

8. To deselect a file within a group of selected files, hold the _____ key and click the highlighted file you want to deselect.

9. To select all files, select _____ from the menu on the toolbar and click **Select All**.

10. _____-click a file to open it.

11. To copy a file or folder onto a floppy disk, _____-click the file and click_____; then click **3 ½ Floppy**.

12. Until you_____ the Recycle Bin, the files are still in the folder on the hard drive.

13. Files can be _____ from the **Recycle Bin** to the original folder that stored the file.

14. _____-clicking the **Recycle Bin** brings up a menu, which allows easy emptying.

Worksheet 5.2.2: Managing Printers

1. To add a new printer, you need to click the **Start** button, go to **Settings**, choose **Printers**, and then select _____.

2. The seven steps to the Add Printer Wizard in Windows 98 are as follows:

    Step 1. Select _____ or _____ printer.

    Step 2. Select the printer _____.

    Step 3. Locate the _____ on the manufacturer and model list.

    Step 4. _____ the new printer, especially if many printers are being used.

    Step 5. Give the printer a _____ name if others on the network need to use it.

    Step 6. Print a _____ page.

    Step 7. If you want, you can set this printer to be the _____ printer, if it is the one most commonly used.

3. You can access the print manager by clicking the _____ icon on the right side of the taskbar.

4. You can access the print manager by going to the _____ folder under **Settings** on the **Start** menu; then _____-click the printer you are using.

5. Sometimes, you will encounter a printer _____; a pop-up _____ appears to let you know what it is.

Worksheet 5.4.2: Hard Drive Preparation

Match each vocabulary word with its correct definition.

1. _____ Primary Partition

    a. The collective name for all tracks having the same number in a hard disk drive when several disks are stacked and rotate on a common spindle

2. _____ Extended Partition

    b. The area on each logical DOS disk where the information to boot the operating system is recorded

3. _____ Active Partition

    c. A special file that is created and located in the disk's sector 0 where DOS stores information about the disk's directory structure

4. _____ Logical Drive

    d. The first partition on a DOS disk (usually contains an operating system)

5. _____ FDISK

    e. A 512-byte chunk of space on a DOS disk

6. _____ Boot Sector

    f. The partition DOS refers to at boot up

7. _____ Partition Table

    g. The process that creates a blank File Allocation Table and root directory structure on a DOS disk

8. _____ Track

    h. A physical separation of information within an extended partition

9. _____ Sector

    i. The process that marks off the disk into sectors and cylinders, and defines their placement on the disk

10. _____ Cluster

    j. The partitioning program for MS-DOS

11. _____ Cylinder

    k. The partition that is normally assigned all the available space left on a DOS drive

12. _____ FAT

    l. Concentric circles on the disk surface created by formatting a hard drive

13. _____ Low-Level Format

    m. Two or more sectors on a single track

14. _____ High-Level Format

    n. A record of the starting point of each logical drive, active partition, and master boot record

Worksheet 5.6.6: Troubleshooting Windows Installation

1. Isolate the problem as either _____ or _____ related.

2. If, after installing the OS and not receiving a successful boot, first attempt to restart the machine by using the _____.

3. To learn more about setup errors, refer to the_____.TXT file that comes with the Windows installation disks or CD.

4. The computer's System Properties gives _____ categories of information, each represented by a tab.

5. The _____ _____ in Windows provides a graphical interface representation of the devices configured in the system.

6. A device _____ is software specially designed to enable the computer to use the hardware or devices installed within the system.

7. What is a Windows startup disk?

_____

_____

_____

_____

8. To create a Windows 98 startup disk, double-click _____ from the Control Panel window.

9. In addition to the critical operating system files copied to the Windows 98 startup disk during creation, what three important disk utilities for troubleshooting are added? (Check three.)

_____	Scandisk.exe	_____	Msd.exe	_____	Mem.exe
_____	Win.com	_____	Autoexec.bat	_____	Format.exe
_____	Win.ini	_____	System.ini	_____	Fdisk.exe
_____	Config.sys	_____	Bootlog.txt	_____	Setup.txt

10. When the Save Uninstall Information option is selected during Windows 98 setup, setup creates the _____ .dat and _____ .ini files that contain the uninstall information.

Lab 6.2.3: Upgrading the Video Accelerator

Estimated Time: 30 Minutes

Objective

Upon completion of this lab, you will be able to install a video card with advanced capabilities such as 3D, more memory, or Accelerated Graphics Port (AGP). Also, you will be able to remove the old video drivers and install new ones.

Equipment

The following equipment is required for this exercise:

- Electrostatic discharge (ESD) wrist strap

- Lab computer with Windows 98 installed

- Standard Phillips head screwdriver that is not magnetic

- AGP video card and driver installation software

- Motherboard manual

Scenario

Your computer either has video capabilities built into the motherboard or has a basic video card installed. You need to install an advanced graphics board to use 3D graphics, to use a larger Desktop, or to use programs that require more video memory.

Procedures

This lab involves working with delicate components inside the computer case that are sensitive to static electricity. After the computer cover has been removed, touch an unpainted metal part of the chassis. Before touching anything else inside the case, be sure the ESD wrist strap is on. If your motherboard has video capabilities built in, be sure to consult the motherboard manual for instructions on disabling this feature in the Basic Input/Output System (BIOS) (or a jumper on the motherboard) before proceeding.

Step 1

Before installing a new adapter, it is typically necessary to change the current video card drivers to basic Windows drivers. To accomplish this, go to **Start** > **Settings** > **Control Panel**. Double-click **System**, click the **Device Manager** tab, and locate the video adapter. Click the + next to the item to show the name of the device. Next, double-click the device to show its properties and click the **Driver** tab and **Update Driver**. When prompted, click **Display a list of all the drivers in a specific location, so you can select the driver you want**, click **Show all hardware**, locate [**Standard Display Adapters**], and install [**Standard VGA 640x480**]. Close any open windows and shut down the computer by clicking **Start Shut Down**; then select the **Shut Down** option and click **OK**.

Next, unplug the computer from the wall outlet to make sure it will not be turned on accidentally. Finally, unplug the monitor cable from the computer.

Step 2

Open the computer case and lay it on its side and locate the expansion slots.

Step 3

Remove the screw holding the expansion card access cover in place. Remove the cover and set it aside.

Step 4

Remove the existing video card from the expansion slot and place it either in an antistatic bag or on an antistatic mat. Next, remove the replacement card from its antistatic bag. Hold the card by the edges, being careful not to touch any of the components on the card.

Step 5

With one hand, grasp the top of the card by the metal end that is attached to the chassis by a screw, and the top corner of the circuit board with the other hand. Next, place the card edge connector into the PCI or AGP expansion slot, depending on the type of video card that you have. Be sure to line up the metal guide on the bottom of the card with the small opening where the expansion card access cover was removed.

Step 6

Using a back-and-forth rocking motion and a little bit of pressure, the card should seat into the socket fairly easily. Do not use too much force to insert the card edge connector. If the card does not seat correctly, remove it and make sure to align everything correctly. Then try again. When the card is properly seated, the metal tab will line up perfectly with the screw hole. Make sure that the card is evenly seated in the expansion slot.

Step 7

Either secure the tab with the screws from the access cover or with the screws provided with the card. Remove the ESD strap from the computer and fit the case back together.

Step 8

After the computer is back together, plug the monitor cable into the new graphics card. Next, plug the computer back into the power outlet and make sure that all connecting cables are secure.

Step 9

Turn on the computer and follow the on-screen instructions. The Windows 9x operating system should find New Plug & Play Hardware and try to install the device drivers for it. When prompted, insert the disk that came with the video card to complete the software installation. Click **Yes** when prompted to reboot the computer for changes to take effect. Typically, with cards that come with a manual, follow the installation instructions of the manufacturer.

Step 10

After the computer has rebooted, the video card should be ready for use. Test the card by changing the resolution of the monitor or run a 3D application.

Troubleshooting

If the resolution cannot be changed to the expected range, or a 3D application will not run, check the device manager to make sure that there is no conflict with the new adapter. Reinstall the standard VGA driver, reboot, and reinstall the new drivers for the video card.

Reflection

What was the most challenging part of this exercise? Why?

_____

_____

_____

_____

_____

_____

_____

_____

_____

_____

Lab 6.3.4: Sound Card Installation

Estimated Time: 30 Minutes

Objective

Upon completion of this lab, you will be able to install a sound card in a computer, attach the speakers and microphone, and install the proper drivers.

Equipment

The following equipment is required for this exercise:

- ESD wrist strap

- Lab computer with Windows 98 installed

- Standard Phillips head screwdriver that is not magnetic

- Sound card and driver installation software

- Speakers

- Microphone

- Motherboard manual

Scenario

The computer either has sound capabilities built into the motherboard or has no sound capability at all. You have decided that you need to add a sound card to enjoy the full capabilities of the computer's multimedia files.

Procedures

This lab involves working with delicate components inside the computer case that are sensitive to static electricity. After removing the computer cover, touch an unpainted metal part of the chassis. Before touching anything else inside the case, be sure that you are using your ESD wrist strap. If the motherboard has sound capabilities built in, be sure to consult the motherboard manual for instructions on disabling this feature in the BIOS (or a jumper on the motherboard) before proceeding.

Step 1

Shut down the computer by clicking **Start** > **Shut Down**; then select **Shut Down** and click **OK**. Next, unplug the computer from the wall outlet to make sure it will not be turned on accidentally. Also, unplug any speakers or microphone from the motherboard if it is equipped with on-board sound.

Step 2

Open the computer case and lay it on its side in front of you, locating the expansion slots. You are now ready to install the sound card.

Step 3

Locate an empty expansion slot, and using your screwdriver, remove the screw holding the expansion card access cover in place. Remove the cover and set it aside.

Step 4

The next step is to remove the sound card from the antistatic bag. Hold the card by the edges, being careful not to touch any of the components on the card.

Step 5

Grasp the top of the card by the metal end that is attached to the chassis with one hand and the top corner of the circuit board with the other hand. Next, place the card edge connector into the expansion slot you have chosen. Be sure to line up the metal guide on the bottom of the card with the small opening where the expansion card access cover was removed.

Step 6

Using a back-and-forth rocking motion and a little bit of pressure, the card should seat into the socket fairly easily. Do not use too much force to insert the card edge connector. If the card does not seat correctly, remove it and make sure to align everything correctly. Then try again. When the card is properly seated, the metal tab will line up with the screw hole. Make sure that the card is evenly seated in the expansion slot.

Step 7

Secure the tab with the screw you used to remove the access cover. If the CD audio cable has not been installed yet, attach it at this time.

Step 8

Remove your ESD strap from the computer and fit the case back together.

After the computer is back together, plug the speakers into the sound card in the port labeled speakers or labeled with a small picture of a speaker. Next, plug the microphone into the port labeled mic or labeled with a small picture of a microphone. Now, plug the computer back into the wall socket and make sure that all connecting cables are secure.

Step 9

Turn on the computer. The Windows 9x operating system should find New Plug & Play Hardware and try to install the device drivers for it. When prompted, insert the disk that came with the sound card to complete the software installation. The sound card should now be ready to use.

Step 10

To test the sound card, click **Start** > **Control Panel**. After the control panel appears, double-click the **Sounds** icon. Click any sound that has a small speaker icon next to it and click the small **play** button next to the preview speaker. If you can hear the sound, the card was installed correctly. If there is no sound, double-click the **System** icon in the control panel and click the **Device Manager** tab.

Search for the sound card in the hardware list. Make sure that the sound card is listed and does not have any conflicts.

Troubleshooting

Double check all connections to the sound card making sure that the plugs are inserted all the way. If the speakers are powered externally, make sure that they are plugged into the wall and turned on. Double-click the speaker icon on the right-hand side of the task bar to bring up the operating system's volume controls. Make sure that the controls are turned up and that none of the controls are muted. If there is a problem in the device manager, remove the sound card from the list and restart the computer. This forces Windows to re-install the sound card into the list and re-install the drivers. Also, if the speakers are not self-powered, you might need to reset a jumper on the sound card to the amplified position.

Reflection

What was the most challenging part of this exercise? Why?

_____

_____

_____

_____

_____

_____

_____

_____

_____

Worksheet 6.1.6: Multimedia Devices

Match each device with its appropriate description:

1. _____ Video Card

    A. Transforms digital information into analog signals and applies them to an audio preamplifier

2. _____ Microphone

    B. Takes pictures and movies that can be broadcast on the Internet or sent to someone through e-mail

3. _____ Speakers

    C. An interface that a computer uses to communicate with a musical instrument

4. _____ Web Cam

    D. A device that reads and writes data to compact disks

5. _____ DVD

    E. A device that inputs and records sounds to a computer

6. _____ Video Capture Card

    F. An integrated circuit card in a computer or, in some cases, a monitor that provides digital-to-analog conversion

7. _____ Sound Card

    G. Changes analog signals into sound waves

8. _____ MIDI

    H. An optical recording media that stores enormous amounts of data

9. _____ CD-RW Drive

    I. A device that records from video sources outside the computer

Worksheet 6.2.5: Video Accelerators

1. RAMDAC is an acronym for _____.

2. The RAMDAC converts _____ signals into _____ signals.

3. The video card receives data from the _____ and sends it to the
   _____.

4. The _____, located on the graphics board, provides video during the
   boot process until the necessary video _____ are loaded by the operating
   system.

5. CRT is an acronym for _____.

6. A CRT uses _____, and _____ to produce
   all other colors.

7. VGA is an acronym for _____.

8. AGP is an acronym for _____.

9. The AGP interface is a variation of the _____ bus design
   that has been modified to handle the intense data throughput associated with 3D
   _____.

10. What is refresh rate?

   _____

   _____

   _____

   _____

   _____

Worksheet 6.3.3: Sound Cards

1. Sound is normally stored in _____-bit and _____-bit formats.

2. The RAMDAC receives the processed _____ information and converts it to an _____ signal.

3. Two computer peripheral devices that send a signal to the sound card are the _____ and the _____.

4. The sound card's quality depends on the number of _____ used to hold each sound sample, or the sample size.

5. Sound cards generally have sampling rates that range from approximately _____ to _____ samples per second.

6. Sound cards use two methods to convert digitally stored sound into realistic analog sound: _____ synthesis and _____ synthesis.

Worksheet 6.4.7: CD and DVD Terminology

1. CD-ROM is an acronym for _____.

2. DVD is an acronym for _____.

3. With a CD-R, data is written _____ on a light-sensitive material by a powerful, highly focused _____.

4. The average storage capacity of a CD-ROM disk is approximately _____ MB.

5. Single-speed drives transfer data at a rate of _____ KB per second.

6. WORM is an acronym for _____.

7. A CD-RW drive labeled 48x24x16 _____ data at 48x, _____ data at 24x, and _____ data at 16x.

8. A typical DVD has a capacity that ranges from _____ GB to _____ GB.

9. Match each recording format with its media:

   1. ____ Yellow Book   a. Interactive CD

   2. ____ Red Book   b. Laser Disk

   3. ____ Orange Book   c. Digital Computer Data

   4. ____ Green Book   d. Digital Music CD

   5. ____ Blue Book   e. WORM Drive CD

Lab 7.1.2: Assigning Permissions in Windows 2000

Estimated Time: 30 Minutes

Objective

In this exercise, you learn how to assign NTFS permissions to folders.

Equipment

The following equipment is required for this exercise:

- Computer running Windows 2000 formatted with NTFS

Scenario

Your boss needs you to create a folder structure and assign permissions to the folders.

Procedures

The ability to manage folders and assign access rights is an important capability of operating systems. This capability helps ensure data integrity by defining the level of user access.

Step 1

Some setup is required to complete this lab: First, create a folder and name it Chemistry. Within the Chemistry folder, create an Experiments and a Laboratory folder. Within the Chemistry\Experiments folder, create a Week3 folder. The LocalUser1 and LocalUser2 user accounts should already be created. In the first part of the lab, assign permissions to folders based on these folders, users, and groups that are created. In the second part of the lab, log on to the system as one of the users and test these NTFS permissions.

The following table shows the final structure that will be created:

Folder Name and Path	Groups	Permissions
Chemistry	Users Group	Read and Execute
	Administrators Group	Full Control
Chemistry\Experiments	Users Group	Read and Execute
	Administrators Group	Full Control
Chemistry\Experiments\Week3	Users Group	Read and Execute
	Administrators Group	Full Control
	LocalUser2	Modify
Chemistry\Laboratory	Users Group	Read and Execute
	Administrators Group	Full Control

Step 2

Log on with the administrator account or with an account that has administrator rights and navigate to the folders that were created according to the scenario.

When you get to your folders, right-click the folder that you want to modify permissions on, and click **Properties**. The Properties box should be displayed for the folder with the General tab view.

Click the **Security** tab.

Step 3

Next, click the **Add** button to add permissions to user accounts or groups. The **Add** button displays the Select Users, Computers, or Groups window. Verify that the correct computer name is entered.

In the Name box, select the name of one of the user accounts or groups that was listed in the scenario, and click the **Add** button. You need to repeat this process for each user account and group that is listed for the appropriate folder in the previously mentioned table.

Step 4

Click **OK** when finished. The Properties dialog box for the folder redisplays.

If the Properties box contains user accounts and groups that are not listed in the scenario, you need to remove them by selecting them and clicking **Remove**.

Step 5

This step specifies the permissions for the folders in the scenario. For all user accounts and groups that are listed for the folder in the scenario, under **Name**, select the user account or group that corresponds to the folder. Under **Permissions,** select the **Allow** boxes or the **Deny** boxes next to the appropriate permissions that are listed for that folder in the scenario.

Click **OK** to save your changes and close the Properties box.

Repeat this procedure and continue to assign permissions for each folder listed in the scenario.

Close all the boxes and log off Windows.

Step 6

Log on as LocalUser and navigate to the Chemistry\Experiments\Week3 folder. Try to create a file in the Week3 folder.

Were you able to create this file? _____

Log off Windows and log back on as LocalUser2; navigate to the Chemistry\Experiments\Week3 folder. Try to create a file in the Week3 folder.

Were you able to create this file? _____

Log off Windows and log back on as Administrator; then navigate to the Chemistry\Experiments folder. Try to create a file in the Experiments folder.

Were you able to create this file? _____

Log off Windows and log back on as LocalUser; then navigate to the Chemistry\Experiments folder. Try to create a file in the Experiments folder.

Were you able to create this file? _____

Log off Windows and log back in as LocalUser2; then navigate back to the Chemistry\Experiments folder. Try to create a file in the Experiments folder.

Were you able to create this file? _____

Troubleshooting

Assigning NTFS permissions can be a confusing task when dealing with large amounts of data that can be spread over large volumes. It is a good idea to keep the process as simple as possible. When a drive or volume is formatted with NTFS, the Full Control permission is assigned to the Everyone group. Change this default permission and assign other appropriate NTFS permissions to control access to the folders and files on the network.

Reflection

Why would you use permissions on a computer?

_____

_____

_____

Lab 7.2.1: Creating Users Accounts in Windows 2000

Estimated Time: 30 Minutes

Objective

Upon completion of this lab, you will be able to create users and groups and assign properties to each.

Equipment

The following equipment is required for this exercise:

- Computer with Windows 2000 Professional installed

Scenario

A coworker needs to use your computer when you aren't at work. Because you have files that you do not want him to access, you decide to set up a user account for him.

Procedures

Being able to create users and then organizing those users into groups is an essential task when working with Windows 2000. A user account enables a system administrator to log in and access the resources of the computer and to have a custom environment to work in. A group is simply a collection of users. In this lab, both users and groups are created.

Step 1

From the Control Panel, select the **Users** and **Passwords** applet. Click the **Advanced** tab; then click the **Advanced** button.

What is the title of the window that just opened?

_____

Step 2

In the Local Users and Groups window, select the **Users** folder in the left windowpane. From the **Action** menu, select **New User**.

What options are available in the New User dialog box?

_____

Step 3

In the New User dialog box, fill out the information for a new user named LocalUser. For the password, use the word **password**. Deselect the box that says **User must change password at next logon** and click the **Create** button.

Using the same process, create a second user named LocalUser2. When finished, click the **Close** button.

Step 4

At this point, test the user account by logging off the current user and logging back in using the username you just created.

Did the user account work properly? _____

If the user account did not log in properly, see the Troubleshooting section.

Troubleshooting

If the user account was not created or if it is disabled, retrace the steps necessary to create a new user account and double-check that everything is set up properly.

Reflection

Why is it necessary to have separate user accounts on a local machine?

_____

_____

Lab 7.2.4: Creating an Emergency Repair Disk

Estimated Time: 20 Minutes

Objective

In this lab, you learn how to create and use an emergency repair disk.

Equipment

The following equipment is required for this exercise:

- Computer system running Windows 2000
- Blank 3 ½" floppy disk

Scenario

You are the system administrator for the XYZ Company, and you need to create an emergency repair disk to use if some of your computer systems crash. Also, you need the disk to repair the file systems if they become damaged.

Procedures

In the first part of this lab, you create the emergency repair disk. In the second part of the lab, you use the emergency repair disk.

Step 1

Run the Backup program. Go to **Start** > **Programs** > **Accessories** > **System Tools** > **Backup**. Click the **Emergency Repair Disk** button on the Welcome tab.

Insert a blank formatted disk in Drive A.

Check the box labeled **Also Backup The Registry To The Repair Directory**.

Click **OK**. Remove the disk and label it emergency repair disk and include the current date.

Step 2

Insert the Windows 2000 CD and boot from the CD.

Press **R** to use the emergency repair disk.

When presented with a Fast or Manual option, press **F** to select the Fast option. Press **Enter** to use the emergency repair disk. Insert the emergency repair disk and press **Enter**.

After the files have been repaired, reboot the operating system.

Troubleshooting

If the disk is not the proper type, there might be some difficulty during the disk creation process. Make sure to use a 3 ½" HD formatted floppy disk.

Reflection

How can knowing how to create an emergency repair disk help in the troubleshooting process?

_____

_____

_____

Lab 7.3.1: Installation Demonstration of Windows 2000

Estimated Time: 90 Minutes

Objective

In this exercise, you learn how to install and run through a Windows 2000 installation step by step.

Equipment

The following equipment is required for this exercise:

- Computer with a blank hard disk

Scenario

You are troubleshooting a computer and have been working on it all day. The file system has become corrupt because the user of the system installed software that was infected with a virus. During installation of the software, the virus deleted all files on the hard drive.

Procedures

In this lab you learn how to install the Windows 2000 Professional operating system.

Step 1

Insert the CD into the CD-ROM drive.

Next, configure the system's Basic Input/Output System (BIOS) boot sequence to boot from the CD first. Keep the CD in the drive and restart your computer.

When the system starts up, watch for the following message: *Press Any Key to Boot from CD*. When it appears, hit any key on your keyboard and boot the system from the CD.

The Windows 2000 Setup screen displays and loads the necessary files, as shown in Figure 1.

Figure 1 — Windows 2000 Setup Screen

This screen displays for a few minutes while it copies the files to the hard drive

The Welcome to Setup screen displays, as shown in Figure 2. Press **Enter** to proceed with the installation.

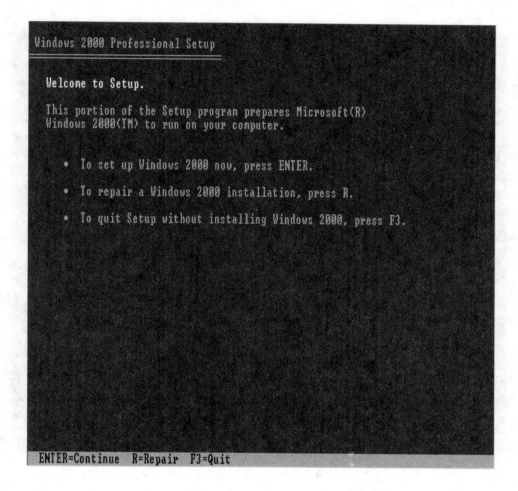

Figure 2 — Welcome to Setup Screen

The Welcome to Windows screen displays. Press **F8** to agree with the Licensing Agreement.

The next step is to partition and format the drive if needed. It is not always required. For this lab, create a small partition (2 GB) for installing Windows 2000. This makes the installation a faster process.

Select the option to partition the drive first, and select the option to format the drive with NTFS.

Setup begins formatting the partition.

When partitioning and formatting is complete, the Windows 2000 Professional Setup screen displays (see Figure 3) and starts copying the system files to the hard drive.

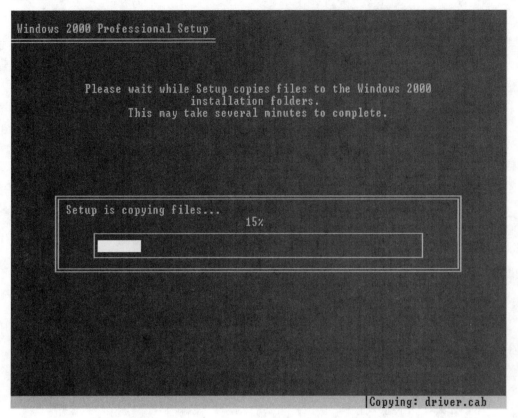

Figure 3 — Windows 2000 Professional Setup Screen

The system restarts automatically when the files have been copied. When the system restarts, the message *Press Any Key to Boot from CD* displays again. This time, you do not want the system to boot from the CD.

The Windows 2000 splash screen displays, as shown in Figure 4.

Figure 4 — Windows 2000 Splash Screen

The Welcome to Windows 2000 Setup screen displays.

Click **Next** to proceed to the Installing Devices screen, as shown in Figure 5.

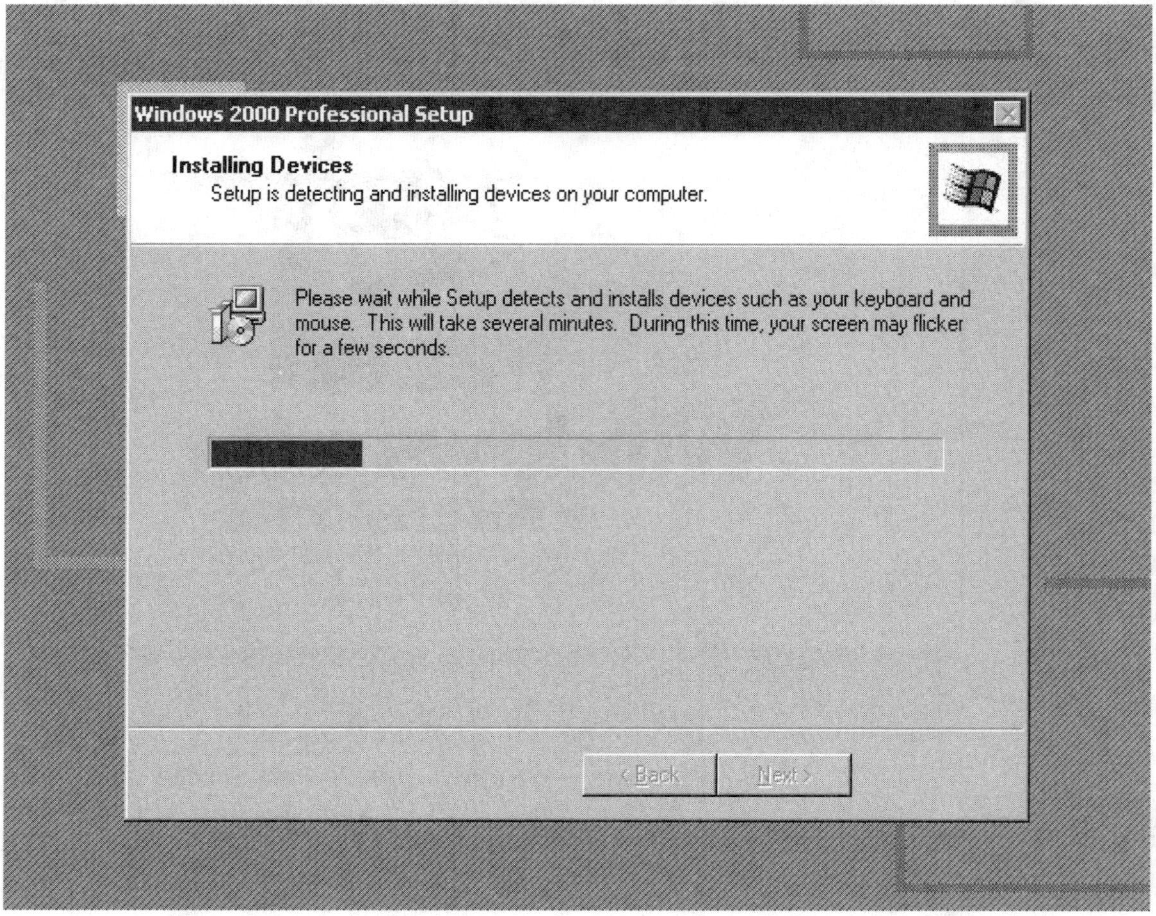

Figure 5 — Installing Devices Screen

When the system finishes installing the devices, setup proceeds to the Regional Setting screen.

You can change these settings if you need to, but for this lab, press **Next**.

On this screen, you enter your name and the name of the company. Click **Next**.

Enter the Microsoft product registration key when prompted. Click **Next** to continue.

The Computer Name and Administrator Password screen displays, as shown in Figure 6. Enter the computer name and the administrator password.

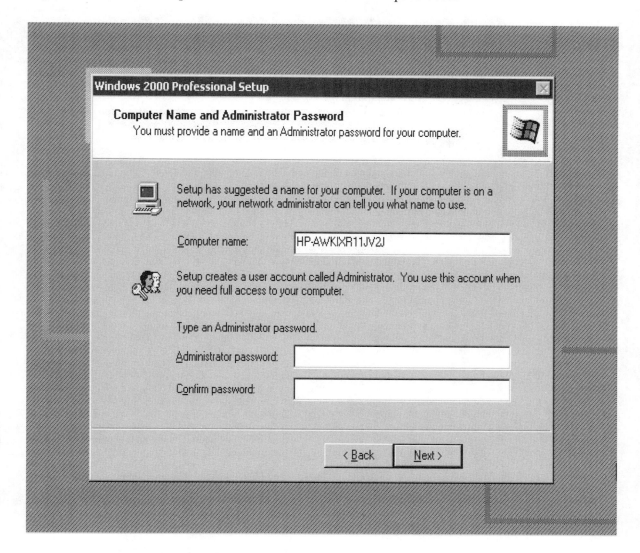

Figure 6 — Computer Name and Administrator Password Screen

Accept the name suggested by setup or enter the name assigned to this computer by the network administrator. Enter the word **password** for the password. Click **Next**.

Enter the appropriate Date and Time settings for your region. Click **Next**.

Setup now proceeds to the Network Settings screen, as shown in Figure 7.

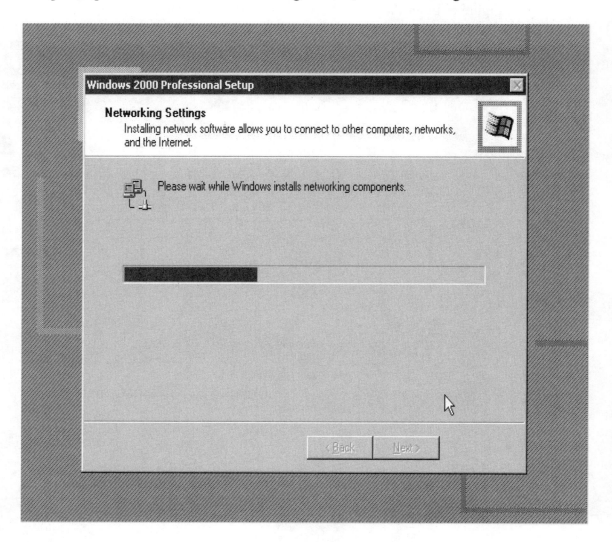

Figure 7 —Network Settings Screen: Screen 1

The networking components are installed during this phase of setup. When complete, click **Next**.

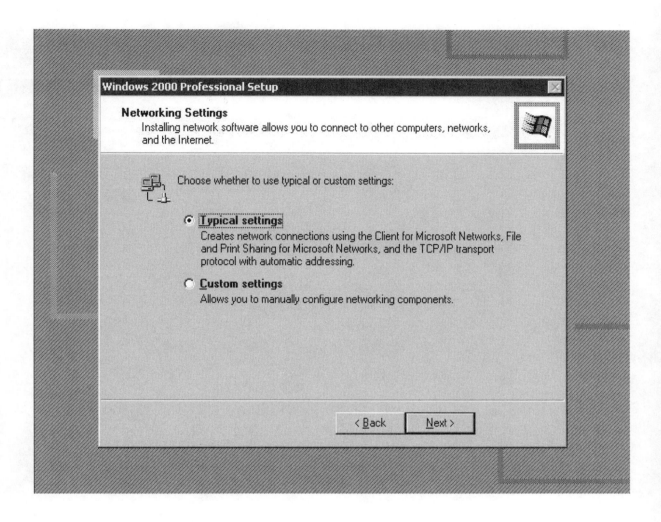

Figure 8 — Network Settings Screen: Screen 2

Select the **Typical settings** radio button (Figure 8) to install the default network settings and click **Next**. Custom settings allows you to install other network components that are not used in this lab.

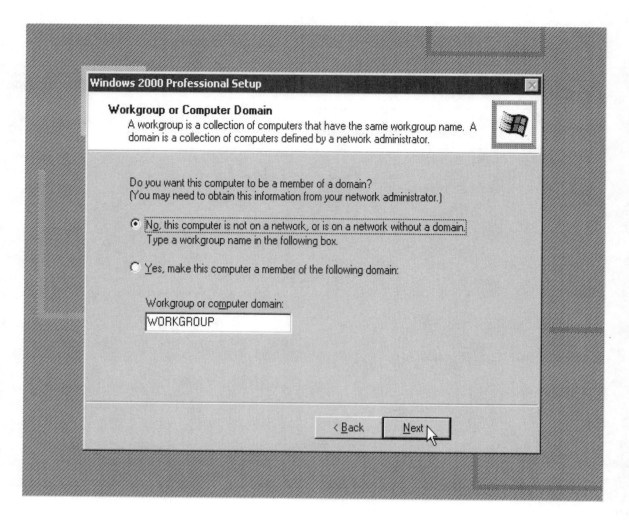

Figure 9 — Workgroup or Computer Domain Screen

The Workgroup or Computer Domain screen (Figure 9) allows you to join a domain. This is important when the computer is on a network and requires a domain name and password.

For this lab, select the **No, this computer is not on a network, or is on a network without a domain** radio button. Click **Next**.

The Performing Final Tasks screen displays (Figure 10).

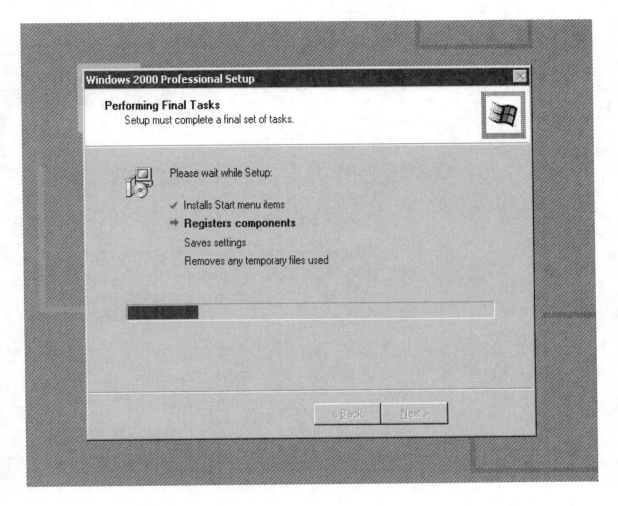

Figure 10 — Performing Final Tasks Screen

This is the final step of the setup process and takes the longest to complete. After it finishes, click **Next**.

The computer automatically restarts. Ignore the *Press any Key to Boot from CD* message and do not boot from the CD.

The Windows 2000 splash screen displays and the Network Identification Wizard starts, as shown in Figure 11.

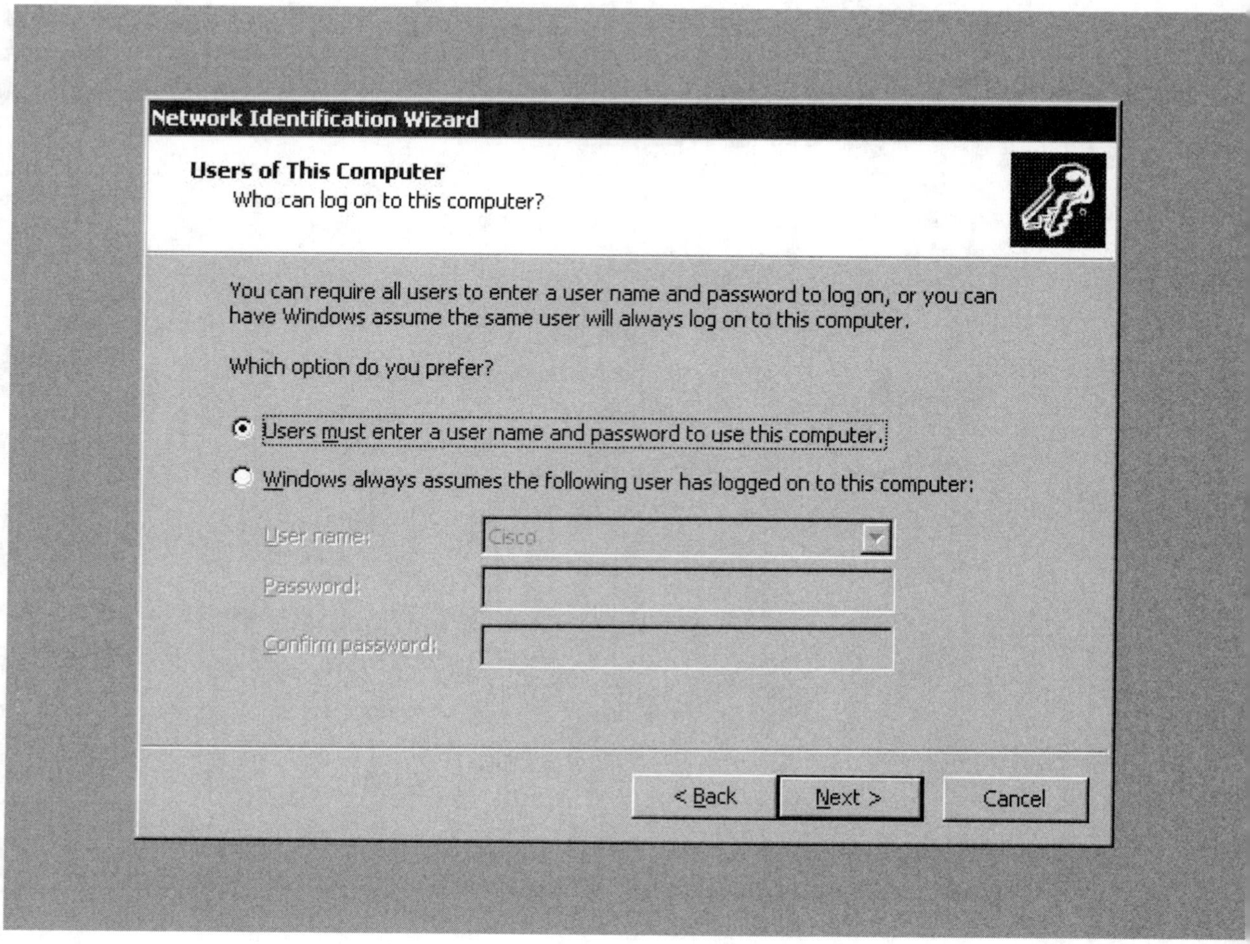

Figure 11 — Network Identification Wizard Startup Screen

Select the **Users must enter a user name and password to use this computer** radio button.

This requires all users to have an account created on the computer before they are allowed to log on. Click **Next**.

To complete the Network Identification Wizard, click **Finish**.

The log on box displays. Log on with the Administrator account and password that you created during setup.

The system now logs you on and launches the Windows 2000 Desktop, as shown in Figure 12.

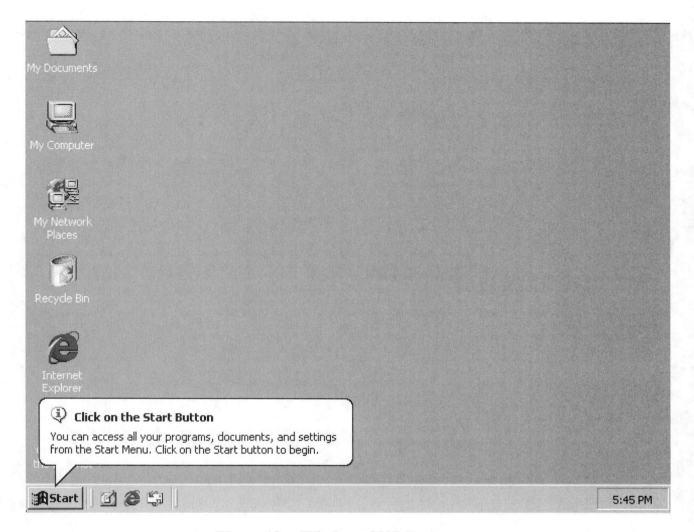

Figure 12 — Windows 2000 Desktop

Windows 2000 has now been successfully installed.

Troubleshooting

Before doing the installation, confirm that you have the proper hardware requirements on your system. Also make sure that you are installing the operating system on a blank partition or hard drive that has enough space. If your hardware is compatible and you have sufficient space on your drive or partition, you should not run into any problems with the installation.

Reflection

Did your Windows installation complete successfully? _____

If you needed to install Windows on another system, do you feel confident that you would be able to? _____

Lab 8.1.2: Basic Disk to Dynamic Disk Conversion

Estimated Time: 20 Minutes

Objective

Upon completion of this lab, you will be able to convert your hard drive from a basic disk to a dynamic disk.

Equipment

You need the following items to complete this lab:

- PC with Windows 2000 Professional installed

Scenario

You want to set up RAID 0 on the new server you just purchased for your home. You are running Windows 2000 Professional as your operating system. You have a 20 GB hard drive and you plan to purchase another one to set up RAID 0.

Procedures

In this lab, you convert your hard drive from a basic disk to a dynamic disk, which enables you to configure RAID 0 striping on your PC.

Step 1

Right-click **My Computer** and click **Manage**.

What window opens when you click **Manage**? _____

Step 2

In the left windowpane, click **Storage**. In the right windowpane, double-click the **Disk Management (local)** snap in.

How many disks do you have on your computer? _____

How many partitions and what are they named? _____

What other devices appear in the window? _____

Step 3

Right-click your local disk (Disk 0) and click **Upgrade to Dynamic Disk.** In the window Upgrade to Dynamic Disk, put a **check** in the box next to Disk 0, if there is not already one, and click **OK**.

Step 4

In the window Disk to Upgrade, verify that it is **Disk 0** and that a **Yes** is underneath where it says *Will Upgrade* that it.

Step 5

In the same window, click **Details** in the lower left corner. What does it say?

_____

Do you have any volumes contained on Disk 0?

_____

Step 6

Click **OK** and you return to the Disk to Upgrade window. Now, click **Upgrade**. A warning window appears asking you if you are sure; click **Yes**. Now, the last warning window appears. Read it and click **Yes**.

Step 7

A window appears saying a reboot will take place to finish; click **OK**.

Step 8

After the computer reboots, it says *Windows 2000 has finished installing new devices. You must restart your computer before the new settings will take effect.* Click **Yes**.

Step 9

Right-click **My Computer** and click **Manage**. Click **Storage** and then **Disk Management (local)**.

Did it convert to a dynamic disk? _____

Troubleshooting

Click **Action** in the upper left corner and click **Restore Basic Disk Configuration**. A warning appears; click **Yes**.

Can you convert back to a basic disk without losing any information? Why?

_____

_____

Reflection

Did any problems occur when converting the basic disk to a dynamic disk?

_____

_____

_____

_____

_____

_____

_____

_____

_____

_____

Worksheet 8.1.3: RAID

1. What is hardware-based Raid?

_____

_____

_____

_____

2. What is software-based RAID?

_____

_____

_____

_____

3. Below each of the following pictures, indicate if it is RAID 0, RAID 1 mirroring, RAID 1 Duplexing, RAID 5, or RAID 1/0.

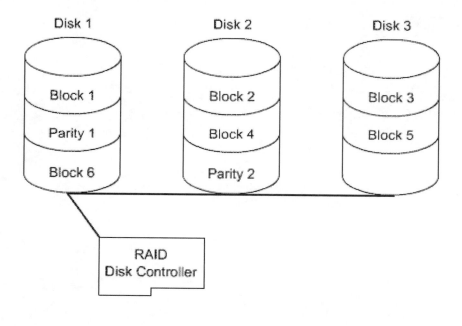

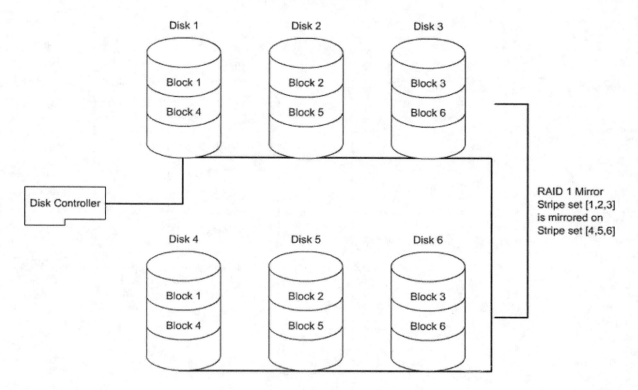

Disks 1, 2, and 3 are RAID 0

Disk 1   Disk 2   Disk 3

Block 1   Block 2   Block 3

Block 4   Block 5   Block 6

Disk Controller

RAID 1 Mirror
Stripe set [1,2,3]
is mirrored on
Stripe set [4,5,6]

Disk 4   Disk 5   Disk 6

Block 1   Block 2   Block 3

Block 4   Block 5   Block 6

Disks 4, 5, and 6 are RAID 0

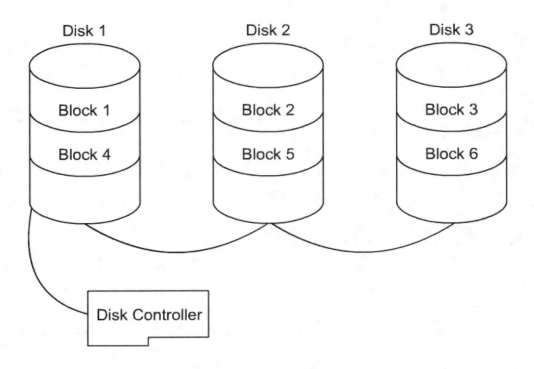

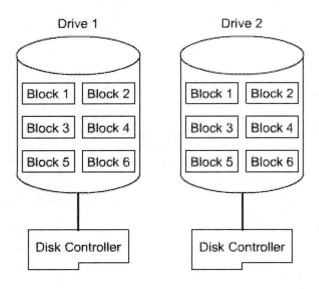

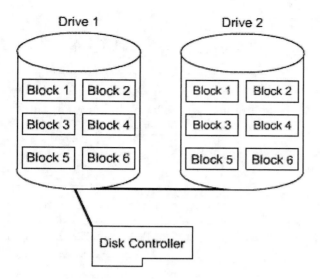

Worksheet 8.3.1: Adding Processors

1. How do you check the motherboard to see if it can support a faster clock speed?

_____

_____

2. To add another processor to a multiprocessor-capable network server, the new processor must meet what criteria? _____

3. The seven steps for adding additional processors are as follows:

Step 1: _____

Step 2: _____

Step 3: _____

Step 4: _____

Step 5: _____

Step 6: _____

Step 7: _____

4. On a Windows NT and Windows 2000 server the _____ must be updated before multiple processors are added.

5. What number from the processor label can you use to look up Intel web sites to identify the processor currently in your network server? _____

6. When upgrading a single processor to a faster single processor, does the BIOS need to be upgraded? True/False _____

7. What two ways is the processor identification utility available?

_____   _____

8. Can Novell support multiple processors? _____

9. What are the steps taken to enable multiple processors in Novell?

_____

_____

_____

10. What must be done in Linux to support multiple processors?

_____

_____

_____

11. What command shows you the current processor information?

_____

Worksheet 8.4.1: Adapters

1. What are the terms that are associated with multiple network interface cards (NICs) in a network server?

   _____, _____,

   _____, _____.

2. What is adaptive or adapter fault tolerance?

   _____

   _____

   _____

3. What is adapter or adaptive load balancing?

   _____

   _____

   _____

4. What allows multiple NICs to act together to increase the bandwidth of a network server?

   _____

   _____

5. When using multiple NICs, should they run at the same speed? Yes/No _____

6. Peripheral Component Interconnect (PCI) hot plug (or PCI hot swap) technology has three capabilities. What are they?

   _____

   _____

7. What commonly used adapter provides onboard memory in a network server?

   _____

   _____

8. How does a Small Computer System Interface (SCSI) adapter use onboard memory?

   _____

   _____

9. Where do the read and write operations take place with SCSI technology?

   _____

10. How is the onboard memory backed up on a RAID controller?

   _____

   _____

Lab 9.3.1: NIC Installation

Estimated Time: 30 Minutes

Objective

In this exercise, you will install a network interface card (NIC) into a PC. You will also configure that NIC to use an IP address.

Equipment

The following equipment is required for this exercise:

- PC with Windows 9x
- NIC with appropriate drivers
- Anti-static wrist strap
- Tool kit
- Windows 98 installation CD or cab files.

Scenario

As a PC technician, you are in charge of installing new hardware. Your manager informs you that they have decided to install a network using their existing PCs. You are asked to install the necessary hardware on each computer that will allow them to be networked.

Procedures

A PC technician is responsible for upgrading and maintaining PCs for the company. As part of this job a technician often upgrades existing PCs with new hardware to fit the company's changing needs. To allow a PC to be networked, one of the first things a technician must do is install a NIC. A NIC allows a PC to access the networking media (cabling) and to communicate with other PCs.

Step 1

To properly install a NIC, it is important to note several items. First, to prevent the NIC from being damaged by electrostatic discharge (ESD), it is important that you ensure that you are properly grounded. Wear an ESD wrist strap that is fastened to the metal frame of the PC whenever you are handling computer components. Also, as you handle the NIC, only hold it by the edges, and do not touch the gold metal contacts along the bottom of the card.

Examine the NIC. Who manufactured the card? _____

Are you able to identify a model number? If so, what is it? _____

Can you identify what speed(s) your NIC operates at? If so, what speed? _____

Looking at the end of the card, what type of media connects to it?

_____

What slot type does your NIC fit into?

_____

Step 2

Now that you have examined the NIC, it is time to proceed with the installation. Make sure that the PC you will be installing the NIC into is shutdown and unplugged.

Remove the cover from the PC. Choose which slot on the motherboard you will be installing the NIC. You might need to remove a small metal cover from the back of the expansion slot for the NIC to install properly. The NIC installs only one way. Make sure it is lined up properly. Also remember that it is possible to damage the NIC or the motherboard if you push too hard or try to force the NIC into place.

After the card is installed, secure the card with a screw, otherwise the card might dislodge when you plug a patch cord in. After you are finished with the card, replace the cover and plug the machine back in.

Step 3

Now that the hardware is installed, it is time to install the software. For this step to be completed properly, you must have the correct driver for your NIC. A driver is a piece of software that allows an operating system to access a piece of hardware, such as the NIC. Depending on the age of your NIC, Windows might already have a driver for it, if not, go to the NIC manufacturer's web site and download it. You can use the information found in Step 1 to ensure that you have the right driver.

Boot your PC.

Did Windows find new hardware? If no, refer to the Troubleshooting section for suggestions. _____

After Windows finds new hardware it brings up the Add New Hardware Wizard screen. Click **Next**. Windows now asks you whether you want to search for the best driver or have Windows display a list of drivers that it includes. Go ahead and choose **Search for the best driver for your device** and click **Next**. You must now specify where the driver is located. If you have it on CD, click **CD-ROM drive**, or if it's on a floppy disk, click **Floppy disk drives**. If you know the exact location, click **Specify a location**, and type in the path to the driver, or click **Browse** and highlight the folder that the driver resides in. After you have made your selection, click **Next**. Windows now shows you the name of the device and where the driver is located. Click **Next** and Windows installs the driver and informs you when it has finished installing the software. You can then click **Finish**, and Windows prompts to reboot. Select **OK** to continue.

Note: Windows might require the Windows 98 installation CD to complete the installation.

Step 4

After you have installed the driver it is a good idea to verify that the NIC was properly installed. To do this, use the following directions.

Right-click over the **My Computer** icon on the Desktop.

Click **Properties**.

Click the **Device Manager** tab.

Click the + sign next to Network Adapters.

Do you see the name of your adapter listed here? _____

Do you see anything else listed here? If so, what? _____

Step 5

Now that you have your NIC installed it is time to set up Transmission Control Protocol/Internet Protocol (TCP/IP).

Right-click **Network Neighborhood**.

Click **Properties**.

Where it says, **The following network components are installed**, scroll down to TCP/IP. If TCP/IP is not listed you need to install it by following the directions below, otherwise skip to Step 6.

Click the **Add** tab.

Click **Protocol** and **Add**.

Click **Microsoft** and scroll down and highlight TCP/IP.

Click **OK**.

You might be prompted for the location of Windows setup files. If you are unsure of their location, ask your instructor for directions.

After you have installed TCP/IP, return to the Network Neighborhood properties and configure the IP address.

Step 6

Double-click the **TCP/IP** listing that also has your NIC listed next to it.

Make sure that you are viewing the IP Address screen, and click **Specify an IP address**.

Enter an IP address and subnet mask that works within your network. You might need to ask your instructor for directions as to which addresses will be used.

After you have entered your IP address and subnet mask, click **OK**.

Click **OK** on the Network screen, and when Windows prompts you to restart, click **Yes**.

Troubleshooting

Occasionally Windows does not detect a new hardware device. If that happens you have to install the device manually.

Click **Start** > **Settings** > **Control Panel**.

Double-click **Add New Hardware**.

Click **Next** to begin installing software for the device.

Click **Next** to let Windows search for new hardware.

If Windows still does not detect the new device, it asks you if you want it to search for a non-plug and play device. You can choose to let Windows search, or you can choose your hardware from a list.

Select **No, I want to select it from a list**.

Click **Next**.

Select **Network adapters**.

Click **Next**.

Select **Have Disk** and specify the location of the driver.

If you still have a problem, shut the computer off and make sure that the NIC is physically installed properly.

Also, a common mistake made by many technicians is accidentally installing the wrong device driver. If this happens, the device usually does not work. The easiest solution is to do the following:

Right-click **My Computer**.

Click **Properties**.

Click **Device Manager**.

Click the + sign next to network adapters and highlight the NIC.

Click **Properties**.

Click the **Driver** tab at the top of the screen.

Click **Update Driver**.

You then need to follow the prompts to install the correct driver.

Reflection

As a group, research and list as many NIC card manufacturers and their web sites as you can.

_____

_____

_____

_____

As a group, research and discuss how a subnet mask is used within a network.

_____

_____

_____

_____

Lab 9.3.3: Configuring the NIC to Work with a DHCP Server

Estimated Time: 10 Minutes

Objective

Upon completion of this lab, you will be able to configure a NIC to use Dynamic Host Configuration Protocol (DHCP).

Equipment

The following equipment is required for this exercise:

- Network created from the previous sections in this chapter with Windows 9x and TCP/IP enabled

- DHCP server accessible on the network

Scenario

Your company informs you that it is expanding its number of users. Because of the number of users, it is no longer feasible to manually enter all the IP addresses. The company is changing to a dynamic addressing scheme and needs you to begin making the necessary changes to the host computers.

Procedures

As a technician or administrator, you have a choice between two types of address management within a network: static or dynamic.

Static addressing requires an administrator to physically enter a unique IP address into each host on the network. The larger the network becomes, the more difficult it can be to keep track of assigned addresses. This is especially true if hosts are changing to new subnets periodically.

DHCP automatically assigns IP addresses to hosts within the network. A DHCP server is configured to automatically assign an address from a range of addresses known as a scope. The hosts request an IP address from the DHCP server, which then assigns a unique address. This enables PCs to move around within a network and have their addresses changed automatically as needed. It also allows the administrator to manage thousands of addresses in the network.

Step 1

View the Network Neighborhood properties as described here.

Right-click **Network Neighborhood**. Click **Properties**.

Is TCP/IP listed as an installed component? If so, what is the name and model number of the NIC it is bound to? _____

Do you see TCP/IP listed with any other items? If so, list those items here:

_____

_____

Step 2

View the settings of TCP/IP, as described below.

Highlight TCP/IP. (Make sure it is the one listed with your NIC.)

Click **Properties**.

Do you currently have an IP address assigned? If so, write down the address along with the subnet mask.

_____

_____

Step 3

Follow the instructions to change your address from being static to dynamically assigned.

Click the radio button labeled **Obtain an IP address automatically**.

Did anything change on the TCP/IP screen? If so, what?

_____

_____

Step 4

Follow the instructions below for saving the new configuration.

Click **OK** on the TCP/IP Properties page.

Click **OK** on the Network Properties page.

Click **Yes** when you are prompted to restart your computer.

You might be asked to insert a Windows disk to install files. If this happens, ask your instructor for further directions.

Step 5

After rebooting your machine, follow the instructions below to verify your new IP address.

Note: Check the lights on the back of the card. These lights blink when network activity is taking place. Blinking lights on the NIC is an indication that you are on the right track to successfully establishing a network connection.

Click **Start** > **Run**.

Type the command **winipcfg** and click **OK**.

Click the **arrow** next to PPP adapter.

Highlight your NIC and click.

Click the tab that says **More Info**.

What is your new IP address and subnet mask?

_____

_____

What is the IP address of the DHCP server?

_____

_____

When was the lease for the address obtained and when does it expire?

_____

_____

Troubleshooting

When configuring DHCP on a client computer, the computer might come back with an error stating that the server is unavailable. If this happens, the easiest solution is to finish rebooting the machine and then follow these instructions.

Click **Start**.

Click **Run**.

Type the command **winipcfg** and click **OK**.

Click the **arrow** and choose your adapter.

Click **Release**, which clears an address.

Click **Renew**, which requests a new address.

The machine should now be able to join the network after rebooting.

Reflection

As a group, try to think of situations where static addressing would be preferred over DHCP.

On your own, try to see if you can find any other commands that would show your IP address under Windows 98 or Windows NT when using DHCP.

As a network or PC technician, you might be required to manage your company's addressing scheme. Static addressing requires a great deal of management on the technician's part. You need to keep track of what addresses are available and which ones are in use. Depending on the size of your network, this might become complicated and time-consuming. DHCP allows you to create a range of addresses and allows a server to determine what address a host receives. If a host is moved to a new network, DHCP assigns a new address without the administrator's intervention.

Lab 9.7.2: Troubleshooting a NIC Using the Ping Command

Estimated Time: 15 Minutes

Objective

Upon completion of this lab, you will be able to use the **Ping** command to test connectivity and troubleshoot problems based on **Ping** command results.

Equipment

The following equipment is required for this exercise:

- Several Windows 9x PCs with networking installed and configured
- One hub or switch
- One PC with Internet access

Scenario

As the PC technician at your company, you often receive calls from users with complaints about the network. You are in your office one morning when a user calls and complains that she is unable to reach anything on the network. Because the user is in an office in another building, you decide to try troubleshooting her problem remotely before visiting her office.

Procedures

When working with computers that have networking installed, you will be asked to troubleshoot a variety of problems. Depending on the size of your company, this can become quite challenging. If your users are spread out across multiple floors, buildings, or even cities, it can become extremely time-consuming to visit every office for every problem. Luckily, certain utilities allow a technician to begin troubleshooting a problem without leaving the office.

A wide variety of troubleshooting tools are available to a technician. Many of these tools can be expensive to purchase. However, a few utilities are free and come with virtually every operating system. One of the most commonly used utilities is the **Ping** command. The **Ping** command tests connectivity between two hosts (PCs). When you ping a device, you send a signal to the device, which then replies back. If the ping is successful, you know that the connection between the two devices is good. If the ping fails, you know that you either have a bad cable or the device itself has a problem.

Step 1

Open a command prompt, as described here.

Click **Start** > **Run**.

Type the word **command** and click **OK**.

Type the command **ping a.b.c.d** (a.b.c.d is the IP address of your NIC).

Did you receive a reply back? _____

How many times did your NIC reply back? _____

How many bytes were used? _____

How much time did it take for a reply? _____

What was the maximum Time To Live (TTL)? _____

Step 2

You can ping a workstation's own NIC by using its IP address or you can use the loopback address. The address 127.0.0.1 is reserved as the loopback address and is not used on the Internet. Instead, the loopback is an address that pings the NIC installed in the workstation you are currently using.

Type the command **ping 127.0.0.1**.

Did you receive a reply back? _____

Are the values for bytes, time, and TTL the same as last time? If not, what changed?

_____

Step 3

If you can successfully ping your own address, and the loopback, you have successfully installed the NIC and TCP/IP. Now, it is time to test whether you can reach other hosts within your network.

Type **ping A.B.C.D**. (This time A.B.C.D is the address of another workstation within your network.)

Did you receive a reply back? If not, what was the error message?

_____

_____

Are the values the same for bytes, time, and TTL as they were in Step 1? If not, what has changed?

_____

_____

Step 4

If you can successfully ping another workstation, that means you have a good connection between the two. There are times, however, when using the **Ping** command can result in a problem.

Type the command **ping A.B.C.D** (A.B.C.D is an IP address for someone outside of your network).

What message did you receive?

_____

_____

What do you think this message might mean?

_____

_____

Now using a PC with an Internet connection, open a DOS prompt and type **ping 1.1.1.1**.

What message did you receive this time?

_____

_____

What do you think this message might mean?

_____

_____

Troubleshooting

If you have trouble pinging the IP address of your workstation, or if you are unable to ping the loopback address, you need to check your TCP/IP settings. If you did not set up TCP/IP properly, you will not be able to ping anything. Check to make sure that you have the protocol installed and that it is bound to your NIC.

If you have trouble pinging other hosts within your own network, check your cable to make sure that it is plugged into the hub or switch. Check your IP address to make sure that you entered it correctly and that the subnet mask is also correct.

Reflection

After a PC is installed on a network, much of a technician's time is spent trouble-shooting network problems. It is important that a technician try to save as much time as possible. **Ping** is a great utility to use when beginning to troubleshoot a problem. **Ping** helps a technician determine whether the network problem is related to a bad cable, an incorrect TCP/IP setting, or a problem with a remote device. Make sure you are comfortable using the **Ping** command and its responses. It will save you a lot of time and energy in the long run.

Worksheet 9.2.5: Types of Networks

1. What is the definition of a network?

_____

_____

2. What is the definition of a computer network?

_____

_____

3. Provide a brief definition for each of the terms:

LAN: _____

_____

WAN: _____

_____

_____

_____

MAN: _____

_____

_____

Circuit-switched network: _____

_____

_____

_____

Packet-switched network: _____

_____

_____

_____

Client/server network: _____

_____

_____

_____

Peer to Peer: _____

_____

_____

_____

Hybrid network: _____
_____
_____
_____
_____

4. On a LAN, what are the rules for coordinating the use of the medium called?
_____

5. Define CSU/DSU:
_____
_____
_____
_____

6. A data channel, over which data can be sent, can operate in one of three ways. Name them:
_____
_____
_____
_____

Worksheet 9.4.2: Network Topology

1. What is the difference between physical topology and logical topology?

   _____

   _____

   _____

2. Describe the following topologies:

   Bus: _____

   _____

   _____

   Star: _____

   _____

   _____

   Extended Star: _____

   _____

   _____

   Ring: _____

   _____

   _____

   Mesh: _____

   _____

   _____

   Hybrid:_____

   _____

   _____

3. What is the definition of networking media?

   _____

   _____

4. What does the term architecture refer to?

   _____

   _____

5. In a token ring implementation, what is the purpose of the monitor of the ring?

   _____

   _____

Worksheet 9.6.5: OSI Model, TCP/IP Protocols

1. What does OSI stand for? _____

_____

2. How does the OSI model work, and include an example: _____

_____

_____

_____

_____

_____

3. Explain the purpose of each of the seven layers of the OSI model:

Application: _____

_____

_____

Presentation: _____

_____

_____

Session: _____

_____

_____

Transport: _____

_____

_____

Network: _____

_____

_____

Data link: _____

_____

_____

Physical: _____

_____

_____

4. What is a protocol? _____

_____

_____

_____

5. For what purpose was the original TCP/IP designed? _____

_____

_____

_____

6. How does TCP/IP differ from the OSI model? _____

_____

_____

_____

7. Explain application protocols: _____

_____

_____

_____

8. Explain transport protocols: _____

_____

_____

_____

9. Explain network protocols: _____

_____

_____

_____

Worksheet 9.8.7: Connecting to the Internet

1. Explain the difference between synchronous and asynchronous:

_____

_____

_____

_____

2. What is the definition of a modem?

_____

_____

3. List the four main types of modems:

_____

_____

_____

_____

4. There are three activities that occur during the local command and online state of a modem. List them:

_____

_____

_____

5. What are AT commands?

_____

_____

_____

6. What does ISP stand for and what role does an ISP play in the Internet?

_____

_____

_____

7. What does vBNS stand for and what role does the vBNS play in the Internet?

_____

_____

_____

8. Explain the major differences between DSL and cable modems:

_____

_____

_____

_____

Lab 10.3.8: Adding an Ink Jet Printer to Your Computer

Estimated Time: 30 Minutes

Objective

In this lab, you connect a printer to a PC, install the correct printer driver, and verify computer/printer communication by printing a test page.

Equipment

The following equipment is required for this exercise:

- Computer with Windows 98 installed
- Inkjet printer with ink cartridges installed
- Communication cable (Universal Serial Bus [USB] or parallel)
- Printer driver(s)

Scenario

As a PC technician, you are responsible for the installation of printers throughout your organization. Your goal is to properly install and configure an inkjet printer with the proper drivers.

Procedures

A printer is one of the essential components of a computer system. Whether it is a laser printer for high-quality text printouts or an inkjet printer for publishing your digital camera photographs, it is important to know how to install a printer.

Step 1

Connect the communication cable to the printer.

What type of cable are you using to connect the printer to the PC (USB or parallel)?

_____

Which end of the cable did you connect to the printer (USB-A, USB-B, DB-25, or Centronics)?

_____

Step 2

Connect the communication cable to the computer.

Which end of the cable did you connect to the computer (USB-A, USB-B, DB-25, or Centronics)?

_____

Step 3

Power on the printer and make sure that it is functioning properly. Turn the computer's power on and log in to Windows.

Step 4

After the initial logon, Windows should detect the printer. If the computer does not find the printer, you can start the Add Printer Wizard by going to **Start** > **Settings** > **Printers**. Then, double-click the **Add Printer** icon.

If Windows finishes loading the Desktop and does not detect new hardware, what might be the cause?

_____

_____

Step 5

Begin the Found New Hardware Wizard by clicking **Next** at the bottom of the window. This wizard leads you through the entire printer installation process.

The next screen in the wizard asks whether the printer is a Local or Network printer. Select **Local** and click **Next**.

This brings you to a window with a list of printer manufacturers and devices. If you have the drivers for the printer, click the **Have Disk** button and browse for the location of the drivers.

What type of media contains the printer driver?

_____

_____

Why are printer drivers rarely located on a floppy disk?

_____

_____

Step 6

Windows searches the selected medium for appropriate printer drivers. Driver files found show up in the Driver File Search Results screen. From this screen, select the proper driver for the printer and choose **Next**.

Why do manufacturers usually include multiple printer drivers on a single CD?

_____

_____

Windows is now installing the printer driver files. You might see an installation progress message during this phase.

What are common device driver file extensions?

_____

_____

Step 7

The next window prompts you for the port that the printer is connected to. If you used a parallel cable, select **LPT1**.

What ports are listed other than LPT?

_____

_____

Step 8

The Add Printer Wizard now prompts you for the printer's name. You can either use the default name suggested by the system or use another name of your choice. The name you choose might identify the type of printer, the printer's location, or anything else that might help you to identify the printer on your local system.

You also have the choice to make this printer your default printer. If you have more than one printer that you can print to, the default printer should be the one used most often.

What name did you give to your printer?

_____

_____

Step 9

The final step is to print a test page. Click **Yes** to print a test page and click **Finish**. Depending on the printer being installed, a printer initialization program might run. These programs set the print orientation, check to see the type of ink cartridge(s) that are installed, and so on.

Step 10

Click **Finish** or **Close** if the wizard has not already closed. When the test page finishes printing, a dialog box appears asking you if the test page printed properly. If it did, click **Yes**. If the results are not readable, click **No** and follow the printer troubleshooter to help solve the problem.

Step 11

Check to be sure that the printer is installed on the computer. From the Windows Desktop, choose **Start** > **Settings** > **Printers**; this opens the Printers folder.

Do you see an icon for the printer you just installed? If not, see the "Troubleshooting" section of this lab.

_____

Which printer is set as the Default Printer? How do you know?

_____

_____

Step 12

Double-click the printer icon. This opens up the printer queue.

Are any print jobs listed in the printer queue? Why not?

_____

_____

Step 13

Right-click the printer icon and choose **Properties**. The printer Properties dialog box opens.

What tabs are available?

_____

List two user-selectable options from a tab:

_____

Step 14

Click the **General** tab. The Print Test Page is near the bottom of the page. Click the **Print Test Page** button.

After clicking the **Print Test Page** button, what question did Windows ask you? How did you answer it?

_____

Step 15

Congratulations. You have successfully installed an inkjet printer on your Windows computer. If you were not able to print a test page, see the "Troubleshooting" section of this lab.

Troubleshooting

If Windows begins the Found New Hardware Wizard but is unable to locate a suitable device driver, check the printer driver media. Also, a newer, updated printer driver might need to be downloaded from the manufacturer's web site.

If you are able to install the printer but unable to print a test page using either method in the lab, check your communication cable. The cable might be in good enough working order to allow the computer to know it is connected to a printer but might not be of enough quality to pass printer data.

You might also need to configure the Basic Input/Output System (BIOS) for the printer to function correctly. Some computers require the parallel port to be set to EPP. To accomplish this, you need to configure your BIOS.

Reflection

What is an advantage of a laser printer over an inkjet printer?

_____

_____

_____

Lab 10.4.4: Setting Up Print Sharing Capabilities

Estimated Time: 20 Minutes

Objective

Upon completion of this lab, you will be able to verify communication between the server and the client, set up the print server, configure the client, and test the client's print capability.

Equipment

The following equipment is required for this exercise:

- Functional network with at least two computers running Windows
- Printer installed on one Windows computer

Scenario

You are the IT support engineer for a small company. The sales department has one single printer connected to one computer. Because the other sales reps need access to a printer, the manager asked you to make the printer available to the entire sales department.

Procedures

The strength of a computer network is the capability to share resources. An example of a resource is a printer. Windows allows users to connect and install a printer on one computer (the print server) and share it with other computers (clients) on the network. This lab guides you through the steps of setting up print sharing by using Windows.

Step 1

On the computer with the printer attached (the server), click **Start** > **Run**. In the Run dialog box, type **Command** and press **Enter**. This opens a command line session window.

Step 2

Type **IPCONFIG** at the command line prompt. This command gives you information about the IP address of the computer.

What is the IP address of the server?

Step 3

On the client computer, click **Start** > **Run**, type **Command**, and press **Enter**. At the command line prompt, ping the server's IP address (example: PING 192.168.10.1).

What is the purpose of using the **Ping** command?

_____

Were the PING attempts successful? If not, ensure that both computers are properly configured and connected to the network.

_____

Step 4

It is important to know the network identification information for the server. To see this information, from the Desktop right-click **My Computer**, choose **Properties**, and select the **Network Identification** tab.

What is the Full Computer Name of the server?

_____

What is the Workgroup of the server?

_____

Step 5

You need to make sure that the print sharing software is installed on the server. To do this, return to the Desktop, right-click **Network Neighborhood**, choose **Properties**, and click the **File and Print Sharing** button. Make sure there is a check next to the **I want to be able to allow others to print from my printer(s)** option. After that is checked, click the **OK** button. Then, click **OK** on the network Properties window. You are prompted to restart the computer. Click **Yes**.

Step 6

Now that the print sharing software is installed, it is time to configure the particular printer for print sharing. From the Desktop, click **Start** > **Settings** > **Printers** to open the Printers folder.

Is the printer that you want to share available in the folder? _____

Step 7

Right-click the icon of the printer that you want to share with the client computer. Choose **Properties** and select the **Sharing** tab.

Step 8

The sharing options make the printer available to clients and give the printer a unique name on the network. Choose **Shared as** and type in a unique name for the printer.

Why must the name for the printer be unique to other printers on the network?

_____

What name did you give the printer?

_____

Step 9

When you finish with the sharing options, click **OK**.

After clicking **OK** and returning to the Printers folder, what has changed regarding the look of the printer icon, and what does this change signify?

_____

Step 10

You are now ready to begin installing the printer on the client computer. On the client computer, click **Start** > **Settings** > **Printers** to open the Printers folder.

Step 11

Double-click the **Add Printer** icon to begin the Add Printer Wizard. This wizard walks you through the process of selecting the shared printer.

Step 12

Click **Next** to get to the printer type screen. On this screen, choose **Network Printer** and click **Next**. This brings you to the wizard that allows you to browse the network for the printer or to enter the path to the printer.

Step 13

On this screen, type in the path to the printer and choose **Next**. The path is for-matted as follows: **server_name\printer_name** where the server_name is the server's Full Computer Name and printer_name is the name you gave the printer.

What is the path to the printer?

_____

After clicking the **Next** button and returning to the Printers folder, do you see an icon for the printer?

_____

Step 14

Congratulations. The printer has been installed on the client computer. Now, test the communication between the client and the printer.

What are two methods for printing a test page from the client computer?

_____

Troubleshooting

If the computer that a printer is connected to is turned off or is removed from the network, the resources that are being shared from that computer are no longer available. Often, it is necessary to have a dedicated print server so that anyone can print to a computer at anytime.

There are various ways of setting up a print server. Some network-capable printers have print servers built into them. Other print servers are small and can be easily hidden between the printer and a desk or wall.

Reflection

Why would a company install a network printer instead of purchasing a printer for every end user?

_____

_____

_____

Lab 10.5.4: Managing Files in a Printer Queue

Estimated Time: 20 Minutes

Objective

Upon completion of this lab, you will be able to open up the printer queue, add jobs to the printer queue, delete a job from the printer queue, rearrange jobs in the printer queue, and purge all jobs held in the printer queue.

Equipment

The following equipment is required for this exercise:

- Computer with Windows 98 installed
- Installed printer (any type of printer will do)

Scenario

As a system administrator of a school, you find out quickly that when the printer does not print a student's document immediately after he clicks the print button, he will click the print button until it does come out. This can lead to massive amounts of wasted resources.

Procedures

In this lab, you learn how to manipulate print jobs held in a printer queue. After placing jobs in the queue, you learn how to delete single jobs, prioritize jobs, and purge the entire printer queue. These skills become necessary when a print job is sent to the queue but is not the correct document that needs to be printed.

Step 1

Each installed printer uses a queue to hold print jobs. This is an area of memory (and hard drive) that feeds information to the printer. Click **Start** > **Settings** > **Printers** to open the Printers folder. Double-click the printer you are using in this lab. This opens up the queue.

Which printer are you using for this lab?

_____

What jobs are currently in the printer queue?

_____

Step 2

In the printer queue menu bar, click **File** and choose **Pause Printing**. This causes the printer queue to hold all print jobs without sending any information to the printer. Minimize the printer queue window.

Step 3

To add jobs to the printer queue, you need to create some documents to print. Click **Start** > **Programs** > **Accessories** and choose **Notepad**.

Step 4

Using Notepad, type in **Document 1** and save it to the Desktop as low.txt.

Step 5

Add this document to the printer queue by choosing **File** > **Print**. Open the printer queue window. (It is minimized and available on the Taskbar.)

Do you see the print job listed in the printer queue?

_____

Who is the owner of the print job?

_____

What is the progress of the print job?

_____

How long will this job stay in the queue?

_____

Step 6

Use Notepad to create and print two more documents. Type in **Document 2**, save it to the Desktop as medium.txt, and print the document. Type in **Document 3**, save it to the Desktop as high.txt, and print the document.

How many jobs are now being held in the printer queue?

_____

Step 7

Sometimes, it is necessary to cancel print jobs while they are being held in the printer queue. In the printer queue window, right-click **medium.txt**.

What options are available in the context-sensitive menu?

_____

Step 8

Choose **Cancel Printing**.

How many jobs are now being held in the printer queue?

_____

Step 9

By default, the printer queue handles jobs using first-in, first-out (FIFO). Sometimes, it is necessary to give priority to certain print jobs. In the printer queue window, drag low to an area below high and release it.

What is the order of the print jobs held in the printer queue?

_____

When the printer is set to resume printing, which print job will the printer queue release first?

_____

Step 10

To delete all jobs held in the printer queue, you can either delete each single job or choose to purge the entire queue. To purge the printer queue, open the printer queue window, choose **Printer** from the menu bar, and click **Purge Print Documents**.

How many jobs are now being held in the printer queue?

Step 11

Choose the **Printer** menu and click **Pause Printing** to release the printer from its paused state. Close the printer queue window and delete the low, medium, and high documents from your Desktop.

Troubleshooting

If you are unable to place jobs in the printer queue using Notepad, check to ensure that the printer queue you are viewing is the queue for the current default printer. Notepad is a simple application and only prints to the default printer.

Reflection

As a network administrator, how would being able to control the printer queue help with the conservation of resources?

_____

_____

Worksheet 10.6.1: Paper Jams

True or False

1. _____Fragments of paper that are torn in the printing process often must be removed from the paper path.

2. _____ Failing parts that drive paper movement can cause paper to crumple or z-fold in the process of moving through the path.

3. _____Paper clumping is when one page sticks to another because the toner was not fused to the paper correctly.

4. _____A paper jam cannot occur when the wrong type of paper is used because the printer will not accept it through the registration rollers.

5. _____Most of the problems in laser printers that require service are rooted in the paper dust that is accumulated in the paper path.

6. _____Because there are static charges present in the laser printing process, dust will not accumulate outside the paper path.

7. _____If there is toner residue on the printer, use a wet towel to clean the affected area.

8. _____Stepper motors are usually trouble free.

9. _____Poor solder connections on stepper motors have caused intermittent operations.

10. ___Few paper jams are caused by improper paper type or weight.

Lab 11.1.2: Using a Digital Multimeter

Estimated Time: 30 Minutes

Objective

This lab concentrates on your ability to identify and record power supply specifications and connector types. It also focuses on the use of a multimeter to safely test and record voltage readings.

Equipment

The following equipment is required for this exercise:

- Personal computer (no peripherals will be needed)
- PC hand tool kit
- Multimeter

Scenario

You are an On-Call Help Desk Engineer for a small computer sales store. A client, who purchased a computer from your company as well as an extended warranty, is having problems with his PC. Based on his description of the PC's behavior, you suspect it is the power supply.

Procedures

For this lab, need to compile power supply information, test procedures, and observe various types of power supply form factors and characteristics. If at any time you are unsure of the procedure, ask your instructor.

Note: This lab deals with electrical power supplies. Proper care should be taken whenever working with a power supply. Also, students should not wear a grounding strap when testing the power supply.

Step 1

Remove the cover of the computer and properly store the screws.

Step 2

Record the following power supply information (found on the power supply's label):

Manufacturer Name	
Model Number	
Operating Range	
Current at 115 V	
Current at 230 V	
Wattage Rating	

Step 3

Sketch the power supply and identify the four main external components of a power supply by labeling them on your drawing.

Step 4

Name the specific type of motherboard connector that your power supply is using.

Step 5

How many large drive connectors are available on your power supply?

_____

Step 6

How many small drive connectors are available on your power supply?

_____

Step 7

Identify the large drive connector leads, and measure their voltage values (Ask your instructor, if you have any questions related to how to proceed with voltage measurements.)

	Lead Color	Expected Voltage	Actual Voltage
1.			
2.			
3.			
4.			

Step 8

Identify the small drive connector leads and measure their voltage values. (Ask your instructor, if you have any questions related to how to proceed with voltage measurements.)

	Lead Color	Expected Voltage	Actual Voltage
1.			
2.			
3.			
4.			

Step 9

Why is it important for a technician to know the different colors and their values?

_____

Step 10

With the multimeter, measure the voltage on each colored wire of the motherboard connectors. Most motherboard connectors have either two connectors or one long connector.

Use the following table to record the lead color and the measured voltage. (*Note*: Do not measure the black leads because they are ground.) Note the meter lead polarity: Red is positive (+) and Black is negative (-).

1. Lead Color	Voltage Reading
2. Lead Color	Voltage Reading
3. Lead Color	Voltage Reading
4. Lead Color	Voltage Reading
5. Lead Color	Voltage Reading
6. Lead Color	Voltage Reading
7. Lead Color	Voltage Reading
8. Lead Color	Voltage Reading
9. Lead Color	Voltage Reading
10. Lead Color	Voltage Reading
11. Lead Color	Voltage Reading
12. Lead Color	Voltage Reading
13. Lead Color	Voltage Reading
14. Lead Color	Voltage Reading
15. Lead Color	Voltage Reading
16. Lead Color	Voltage Reading
17. Lead Color	Voltage Reading
18. Lead Color	Voltage Reading
19. Lead Color	Voltage Reading
20. Lead Color	Voltage Reading

Step 11

Check the continuity from the ground of the power cord socket to the metal base of the computer.

Step 12

Check the continuity of all three conductors of a power cord from the plug end to the female end.

1. Neutral _____

2. Hot _____

3. Ground _____

Step 13

Why measure voltage when troubleshooting a power supply?

_____

Troubleshooting

One way to determine if a power supply is not functioning properly is to compare the test results from what the connector should be reading. A malfunctioning power supply should not be opened. Replace the component with a new one of the same power capacity.

Reflection

What did you learn from this lab that you did not know before?

_____

_____

How can what you learned here help you in the future?

_____

_____

Lab 11.3.5: Cleaning Computer Components

Estimated Time: 25 Minutes

Objective

Upon completion of this lab, you will know the proper procedures to clean computer components.

Equipment

The following items are needed to complete this lab:

- Computer with a keyboard, mouse, and monitor
- Mild detergent (a little soap, a lot of water)
- Cleaning rag
- Container for the detergent (bucket or spray bottle)
- Can of compressed air
- Tool kit
- Keyboard cap puller (optional)

Scenario

As a PC repair technician, you have been sent to fix a computer that stopped working. A good practice when repairing PCs is to clean the computer before you leave it.

Procedures

When cleaning electrical components, it is critical that you unplug the device before working with it. If there is power running to a computer system when you run a damp cloth over it, the results could be deadly.

Step 1

The first thing that should be cleaned is the inside of the computer case. To begin, unplug the power cord if it is not already unplugged. Next, remove the case cover either by removing the appropriate screws or latch. When the case is open, it is a good idea to keep the case standing vertical or even angled so that when you blow the dust out, it doesn't settle back inside.

Review the precautions and directions on the side of the air can. Use the air sparingly to blow the dust out of the power supply and off all visible surfaces inside the case. After all surfaces are clean, re-attach the case cover.

Has the inside of the case been thoroughly cleaned? _____

Step 2

When cleaning the monitor, the first and most important step is to turn off the unit and unplug it from the wall. After it is unplugged, it is safe to clean the surfaces with a cloth that is dampened with a mild detergent. If the cloth leaves streaks on the screen, there is too much liquid. A damp or moist cloth has only enough cleaner to help remove dust and clean the surface. Using a dry cloth, wipe down the screen and sides to remove any residual cleaning fluid.

When all sides of the monitor have been cleaned, it is a good idea to let it sit and dry for at least a half hour, just in case something might have dripped inside.

Has the monitor been thoroughly cleaned? _____

Step 3

The keyboard is the one computer component that has the most physical contact with the user. Two areas of the keyboard should be cleaned: the surface of the keys and the area below the keys.

The fastest way to remove dust and other loose objects from below the keys is to blow it out with a can of air. Start at one side of the keyboard and work toward the other side until the dust buildup is removed.

Step 4

If a liquid such as soda was spilled on the keyboard, the keys need to be removed in order to clean it out. Using a keyboard cap puller, remove the keys in the area where the spill occurred and use a cloth to clean the mess. When thoroughly cleaned, the keys can be replaced by positioning them in the correct spot and then pressing them down.

Has the keyboard been thoroughly cleaned? _____

Step 5

The mouse is one of the most frequently cleaned components on a computer. The optical mouse requires less cleaning than a mechanical mouse.

To clean a mechanical mouse, remove the locking ring on the bottom. The proper direction to turn the ring should be indicated by an arrow. After it is removed, turn the mouse over to catch the ring and ball.

Observe the two posts that are inside the mouse: the x-axis and the y-axis. If a buildup of dirt is on either one of these, use a Q-Tip and some alcohol to remove the dirt.

Step 6

After the dirt is removed from the posts, inspect the ball to make sure it is clean. If it needs to be cleaned, use a clean rag to polish off the dirt. After it is clean, put the ball back into the mouse and return the ring to the locked position.

Has the mouse been thoroughly cleaned? _____

Troubleshooting

If dust builds up in a power supply, it can cause it to malfunction or shut down. If the fans stop and the system overheats, internal components can be damaged. Preventive maintenance can prolong the life of not only the power supply, but also the entire system.

Reflection

How often should a computer system be entirely cleaned?

_____

Why should computer systems be cleaned?

_____

_____

_____

Lab 11.4.1: Using the Scandisk and Defrag Utilities

Estimated Time: 30 Minutes

Objective

Upon completion of this lab, you will be able to scan a hard drive and defragment the drive to check for errors and to defragment files using the Scandisk and Defrag utilities.

Equipment

The following equipment is required for this exercise:

- Computer with Windows 98 or 2000 Professional installed

Scenario

As a system administrator, your manager expects you to perform routine maintenance on all computer systems as necessary. Run the Scandisk and Defrag utilities on the appropriate machines to keep them running smoothly.

Procedures

If a computer is used on a regular basis and system maintenance is not performed, system stability decreases. As files are created, used, and deleted, the media they are stored on can become fragmented. Also, if a file is not properly closed, it can leave corrupted pieces of data behind. To resolve these problems, two utilities are included with Windows: Scandisk and Defrag.

Step 1

The first utility to run is Scandisk. This utility ensures that any problem files will be fixed before the Defrag utility organizes the drive. To start the Scandisk utility, open **My Computer** and right-click the drive to check; then choose **Properties**. Select the **Tools** tab and click the **Check Now** button. This starts the Scandisk utility.

What types of tests are available in the Scandisk program?

_____

Which test type is the default?

_____

Step 2

To begin the scanning, click the **Start** button. When it finishes, click the **Close** button. If there are errors, see the "Troubleshooting" section of this lab.

Step 3

After Scandisk has completed successfully, the Defrag utility can be run to reorganize the files on your disk. To start the Defrag utility, open **My Computer** and right-click the drive to defrag; then choose **Properties**. Select the **Tools** tab and click the **Defragment Now** button. This starts the Defrag utility.

Note: Make sure that the screensaver and any other program that automatically starts on its own is temporarily disabled or it will interrupt the defragmenting process.

Troubleshooting

If Scandisk reports a cross-linked file or fragments of a file, it might ask you how it should resolve the problem. There is an option to convert recovered data to a text file; however, this clutters the drive with many text files of garbled information. Select the option to discard the information and continue.

Reflection

List any other utilities that come with Windows that can help in the preventative maintenance of a system:

_____

_____

_____

_____

_____

Worksheet 11.1.3: Environmental Considerations

1. Explain why batteries need special disposal guidelines:

_____

_____

_____

2. Explain why monitors need special disposal guidelines:

_____

_____

_____

3. Explain why chemical solvents and aerosol cans need special disposal guidelines:

_____

_____

_____

4. Inkjet printer cartridges and laser printer toner cartridges can be_____ and
_____.

5. OSHA is an acronym for _____.

6. MSDS is an acronym for _____.

7. What is the MSDS used for?

_____

_____

8. MSDS contains information on?

   a. _____

   b. _____

   c. _____

   d. _____

Worksheet 11.2.1: ESD

1. ESD is an acronym for _____.

2. Most computer chips run on less than _____ volts of electricity.

3. Always use _____ to temporarily store computer parts and components until you reinstall them.

4. Devices such as grounding _____ attach you to an earth ground, which gives a place for the static to go before it attacks a sensitive computer component.

5. When the humidity is_____, the potential for ESD increases dramatically.

6. If the temperature is cool or if carpeting is on the floor, there is a _____ potential for static electricity.

7. When you work on a computer, one of the first things you should do when the case has been opened is to _____ yourself to the case by touching an exposed unpainted metal part of the computer case.

8. A good working area should have a climate control system that maintains the relative humidity between _____ percent and _____ percent.

9. If you are working on high voltage equipment, such as a power supply or a CRT monitor, a _____ should not be used.

Worksheet 11.3.5: Preventive Maintenance for Components

1. The majority of preventive maintenance is _____.

2. A problem with dust is its capability to be_____ charged.

3. If the wrong types of cleaners are used, damage from _____ could occur over time.

4. _____ can be a useful tool to quickly and easily clean out a dusty computer.

5. To fully protect your files from virus infection, the virus _____ list must be up to date.

6. If you are going to work on a laser printer that has been in use, let it _____ for a while before coming in contact with the internal components.

7. Define the following terms:

   a. Blackout: _____
   _____
   _____

   b. Brownout: _____
   _____
   _____

   c. Electrical Noise: _____
   _____
   _____

   d. Spike: _____
   _____
   _____

   e. Surge: _____
   _____
   _____

   f. Surge Suppressor: _____
   _____
   _____

   g. Standby Power Supply: _____
   _____
   _____

   h. Uninterruptible Power Supply: _____
   _____
   _____

Lab 12.1.7: The Steps of the Troubleshooting Cycle

Estimated Time: 25 Minutes

Objective

Upon completion of this lab, you will be able to describe the importance and identify the steps involved in the troubleshooting cycle.

Equipment

This is a written lab. No equipment is necessary.

Scenario

You have just started a new job as a computer technician with a small consulting group. The company has approximately 50 employees with varying levels of computer expertise. As a computer technician, your primary responsibility is to provide desktop support to these employees.

You have recently gone through job orientation and have received training on the procedures for responding to computer problems. The training included an introduction to the hardware and software in use, common errors, common symptoms, and using the troubleshooting cycle to effectively solve problems. You consider the training informative and, coupled with your previous computer experience, you are confident in performing your job duties.

The end user is complaining that his computer stopped responding. It is your responsibility to troubleshoot and resolve this problem.

Procedures

The troubleshooting steps can be useful in solving computer problems. Sometimes, a problem requires common sense and the solution is straightforward. Other times, the solution requires a broad level of technical knowledge. In this lab, you walk through the troubleshooting cycle as an example of solving computer problems. The lab begins with step one, which is gathering information from the end user.

Step 1

After arriving on scene, you begin the troubleshooting cycle by defining the problem. Start by identifying the general symptoms and then determine the possible causes for the existing problem.
For future reference, you brought along a notebook to document your findings.

Upon arrival, what environmental factors can you assess? How is an assessment of the environment beneficial?

_____

_____

Step 2

The next step is to gather pertinent information from the end user. Initially, you should ask general questions with the goal of obtaining a broad idea about the computer problem. Your questions will gain focus as information is obtained from the end user.

What questions could be asked to obtain a broad idea about the problem?

_____

_____

After questioning, you learn that the computer is not producing any sound. Everything else appears to be functioning correctly.

You can now assume that the problem is related to the multimedia (sound) capabilities of the computer. What questions could you ask or actions could you take to better define the problem?

_____

_____

During questioning, you find out that the end user has been having problems ever since a recent sound card upgrade. You attempt to reproduce the error by playing an audio file. Sure enough, the audio does not produce any sound. You inspect the audio player, and it appears to function correctly. Next, visually inspect the speaker cables and verify that the speakers are turned on. You see no apparent problems with the connected devices and the speakers are turned on.

Gathering information is by far the most important step of the troubleshooting cycle.

Step 3

Given the above scenario, what are the most likely causes of the malfunctioning soundcard?

_____

_____

The user has stated that he is having problems producing sound from his machine, and there has been a recent upgrade performed on his soundcard. From this information, you can infer that the problem is related to the recent upgrade of the sound card.

You verified that both the audio player and speakers are functioning properly. You also verified that the speakers are connected correctly. Because you verified that the speakers and audio player are working, you figure it is unlikely that they are causes of the problem. You continue the troubleshooting cycle by creating solutions for the apparent bad sound card installation.

Step 4

Effectively developing a solution involves gathering correct information, knowledge of the computer components, and the ability to recognize symptoms.

The problem has been isolated to a bad installation of the sound card.

Give an example of a solution that might solve this user's problem:

_____

_____

Your solution should focus around the different aspects of the sound card installation. Based on your experience, you are aware that most sound card problems result from a bad or outdated driver, improperly installed sound card, or system resource conflicts.

For example, a sample solution might include verifying proper installation of the sound card in the PCI slot. If the problem still exists, you need to check for system resource conflicts. Finally, you need to update or reinstall the driver.

Step 5

The first aspect of your solution involves simply checking the installation of the soundcard.

What precautions need to be taken before working inside the computer case?

_____

_____

You verify that the soundcard has been properly inserted and has good connections. It appears to be properly inserted. Your experience has told you to check for obvious solutions first. If the problem still exists, move onto the second aspect of your solution, which is to check for any system resource conflicts.

The user is running Windows 98, and you check resource conflicts in the Device Manager.

In the Device Manager for Windows 98, what indicates a system resource conflict?

_____

_____

You do not notice any problems and move on to updating or installing the device driver for the sound card. To get the latest device driver for the sound card, you visit the web site for the sound card manufacturer. You conduct a search for the sound card driver and locate a new driver. This driver is different from the one the user installed because it includes a Windows 98 patch that resolves known compatibility issues. You install the new driver and then reboot the machine.

Step 6

The fifth step is determining if the problem has been solved. If the problem appears to be solved, the troubleshooting process has been successfully completed. If the problem is not fixed, you will be required to return to previous steps and to continue the troubleshooting process. Sometimes, it might be necessary to undo changes made to the system and revert to the old configuration. In either case, be certain to properly document your results. Documenting your results helps you work more productively in the future.

After bootup, you play an audio file and hear sound out of the speakers. The problem has been resolved, and the troubleshooting cycle has come to an end.

Troubleshooting

What are the steps in the troubleshooting cycle?

Step 1 - _____

Step 2 - _____

Step 3 - _____

Step 4 - _____

Step 5 - _____

Reflection

It has been stated that troubleshooting is cyclical. What does this mean?

_____

_____

Why are the steps in the troubleshooting cycle useful for solving computer problems?

_____

_____

What is the most important step in the troubleshooting cycle, and why is it so important?

_____

_____

If the problem exists after the solution has been implemented, what steps should be taken?

_____

_____

Lab 12.2.3: Identifying POST Errors

Estimated Time: 20 Minutes looks good

Objective

Upon completion of this lab, you will be able to identify common power-on self test (POST) errors. The ability to identify POST errors is essential for troubleshooting computers.

Equipment

The following equipment is required for this exercise:

- Operating computer
- Mouse
- Keyboard

Scenario

You are a technician for a small medical billing office. The office just bought new computers. The newly purchased computers are the same make and model. You are familiarizing yourself with the computer, and you want to document the POST errors for the major components.

Procedures

To become familiar with POST errors, remove several key components from the computer system and listen for the audible POST errors. POST errors are a series of beeps that indicate a failure during startup. If you hear a POST error, you will then document your findings.

Note: POST errors are dependent on the Basic Input/Output System (BIOS). POST errors are not the same universally.

Step 1

First, remove the keyboard connector from the back of the computer case, and reboot the system. Listen for any abnormal beeps during startup.

Did you hear a POST error?

_____

If you did hear a POST error, what was the pattern of the beep?

_____

Note: If you hear one beep during startup, this indicates normal operation.

Step 2

Plug the keyboard connector back into the back of the computer case. Next, unplug the computer and remove the computer case to expose the internal components. Identify the random-access memory (RAM) on the motherboard and remove the RAM stick(s). Reboot the machine and listen for POST errors.

Did you hear a POST error?

_____

If you did hear a POST error, what was the pattern of the beep?

_____

Step 3

Replace the RAM and reboot the machine. One beep should be heard, which indicates normal operation during the boot process. If any POST errors are heard, verify that the RAM was properly replaced and try again.

Step 4

After the machine boots normally, power off and unplug the computer. Identify and disconnect the floppy drive. Remove the connectors for both the ribbon cable and the power supply that connect to the floppy drive. Reboot the machine and listen for POST errors.

Did you hear a POST error?

_____

If you did hear a POST error, what was the pattern of the beep?

_____

Step 5

Unplug the computer, reattach the floppy drive connectors, and reboot the machine. One beep, which indicates normal operation during the boot process, should be heard. If any POST errors are heard, verify that the floppy drive has been properly connected and try again.

Step 6

After the machine boots normally, power off and unplug the computer. Identify and then remove the video card from the motherboard. Reboot the machine and listen for POST errors.

Did you hear a POST error?

_____

If you did hear a POST error, what was the pattern of the beep?

_____

Step 7

Unplug the computer, replace the video card, and reboot the machine. One beep should be heard, which indicates normal operation during the boot process. If one beep is heard, replace the computer case. If a POST error is heard, verify that the video card was properly replaced and try again.

Troubleshooting

Computer technicians need to be familiar with POST errors and their implications. Technicians need to be aware of any unusual sounds during the boot process because it could be an indication of a failure during initial diagnostic tests. In many cases, these atypical sounds are the first sign that a failure has occurred.

Reflection

When will POST errors occur?

_____

What sound is made during a normal boot process?

_____

Are POST errors dependant on the BIOS installed?

_____

Worksheet 12.1.2: Troubleshooting Basics

1. Troubleshooting is a process of diagnosing a _____ and finding and implementing the correct _____, which results in restoring the system to its original operational state.

2. Fill in the blanks the troubleshooting cycle:

   a. _____ the problem.

   b. Gather _____.

   c. _____ a solution.

   d. _____ a solution.

   e. Is the problem solved?

      Yes. You're done.

      No. Undo changes and _____ Steps 1—4.

   f. _____

3. Why is using the structured approach, provided by the troubleshooting cycle, beneficial in solving computer-related problems?

   _____

   _____

   _____

   _____

   _____

   _____

Worksheet 12.3.2: Troubleshooting Printers

True or False:

1. _____ Problems with dot-matrix printers related to the print quality are some of the most difficult to identify.

2. _____ Because dot-matrix printers are relatively simple devices, only a few problems usually arise.

3. _____ With dot-matrix printers, a common cause of a paper jam is a piece of paper that has torn off and lodged in the paper path.

4. _____ Stepper motors are not sensitive to stray voltages.

5. _____ In a dot-matrix printer, lines of print are unevenly spaced if the main motor is damaged.

6. _____ Print quality is the most common problem associated with inkjet printers.

7. _____ Black lines present in every line of text on a printed page are caused by a plugged hole in at least one of the small pinhole ink nozzles in the print cartridge.

8. _____ Failure of the high-voltage power supply (HVPS) is not the cause of a laser printer printing blank pages.

9. _____ If toner is inside the toner cartridge, you can hear it when it is shaken.

10. _____ The corona wire (or roller) is an inexpensive part and can be easily replaced.

11. _____ Because the drum is grounded, it has no charge and nothing with a charge (such as toner) sticks to it.

12. _____ Toner spilled inside the printer or by a crack or chip in the EP drum can cause repetitive marks.

13. _____ Foreign matter caught on the transfer corona wire causes vertical white lines running down the printed page.

14. _____ Image smudging is caused by a fuser problem.

Worksheet 12.3.4: Troubleshooting Hardware

1. What is a Field Replaceable Unit (FRU)?

_____

_____

_____

_____

2. What is POST used for?

_____

_____

_____

_____

3. Describe what Beep Codes indicate.

_____

_____

_____

_____

4. Explain one main reason for a CPU failure.

_____

_____

_____

_____

5. What is the first place you should check when troubleshooting memory?

_____

_____

_____

_____

6. How can you tell if you have a motherboard problem?

_____

_____

_____

_____

7. List two types of video problems:
   a. _____
   b. _____

8. The first three steps when diagnosing any disk drive problems are the following:

   a. Check the _____ cable.

   b. Check the _____ cable.

   c. Check the device _____ .

9. Most sound card problems are _____ conflicts.

Lab 13.7.4: Booting into Safe Mode

Estimated Time: 25 Minutes

Objective

Upon completion of this lab, you will be able to boot the PC using the advanced troubleshooting options of Windows 2000.

Equipment

The following equipment is required for this exercise:

- Operational computer that is running Windows 2000

Scenario

You are unable to boot a computer into the normal Windows Desktop environment. Boot into Safe Mode to attempt to troubleshoot the problem.

Procedures

Booting the computer into Safe Mode bypasses the normal startup sequence of Windows. Part of this process involves timing. When the black-and-white Starting Windows bar is on the screen, press the **F8** key before the system begins loading Windows; otherwise it is too late.

Step 1

Power on the computer.

Step 2

When the computer is running through the boot process, a series of different startup screens displays. To get into Safe Mode in Windows 2000, press **F8** while the black-and-white Starting Windows bar appears at the bottom of the screen. The Starting Windows bar displays after the Basic Input/Output System (BIOS) has been loaded.

What is the name of the menu that displays?

_____

What are the options that are available on this menu?

_____

Step 3

Next, select the **Safe Mode** option and press **Enter**. Windows loads to the Safe Mode environment. Read the window carefully and press **OK**.

Step 4

Windows loads into the Safe Mode Desktop environment. However, because Windows loads only basic drivers in Safe Mode, the graphics are in VGA mode.

Does the Desktop appear to be in VGA mode?

_____

How do you check the video settings?

_____

_____

Step 5

Next, access the Device Manager to check loaded drivers. To access the Device Manager, click **Start Menu** > **Settings** > **Control Panel** > **System** > **Hardware** > **Device Manager**. The Device Manager opens displaying the hardware components.

Step 6

After the Device Manager is open, check to see if any devices are conflicting. Conflicting devices have a yellow exclamation point next to them.

Are there any conflicting devices?

_____

Step 7

Next, verify that no network drivers have been installed. To verify the network drivers, click the + sign next to Network Adapters. A list of devices should display. Right-click a device, select **Properties**, and a device Properties window appears.

What does the device Properties window display for Device Status?

_____

_____

Troubleshooting

Booting a PC into Safe Mode is often used by computer technicians when troubleshooting a problem. Safe Mode helps technicians identify and diagnose problems. If the problem is not present in Safe Mode, it is probably related to settings or drivers.

Safe Mode loads only generic drivers during the loading of the operating system (OS). It loads basic drivers for the mouse, video display, mass storage, keyboard, and default services. Also, booting a PC into Safe Mode does not network devices/connections by default. However, the PC can be booted using the Safe Mode with Networking to establish a network connection.

Reflection

What key is pushed to enter into Safe Mode in Windows 2000?

_____

What is the main difference between Safe Mode and normal operation?

_____

Why might Safe Mode be an effective troubleshooting tool?

_____

Lab 13.7.5: Using the Windows 2000 Recovery Console

Estimated Time: 30 Minutes

Objective

In this lab, you learn how to use and implement the Windows 2000 Recovery Console.

Equipment

The following equipment is required for this exercise:

- Computer system running Windows 2000

Scenario

You are the system administrator for the XYZ Company, and upon arriving at work in the morning, you have a call from an end user stating that she is receiving a system boot failure. To fix the problem, run the Windows 2000 Recovery Console to repair any boot file that might be damaged.

Procedures

In the first step of this lab, the system boot failure needs to be created. (Don't worry, it will be repaired in the other parts of the lab.) In the second step of the lab, the Recovery Console repairs the system boot failure that was created in the first step. In the third part of the lab, the Recovery Console is installed and some of the Recovery Console commands are used.

Step 1

First, turn off/disable system protection. To do this, left -click **My Computer** and select **Tools > Folder Options**.

In the Folders Options display box, click the **View** tab.

With the View tab selected, change the defaults for viewing hidden and system files. To do this, check the **Show hidden files and folders** radio button. Also, uncheck **Hide protected operating system files (Recommended)**.

Next, rename the Ntldr file to Oldntldr. To do this, click **Start > Search > for Files and Folders**. In the Search for files and folders named, type **Ntldr**.

When the file appears on the right screen, right-click the file and select **Rename**. Rename it to **Oldntldr**.

Restart the computer. An error message should be received when you restart the computer.

Step 2

Make sure that the Windows 2000 installation CD is in the CD-ROM drive and restart the computer. Change the BIOS settings to boot from the CD.

When the Setup Notification message appears, setup now displays the Welcome To Setup screen.

Press **R** to repair a Windows 2000 installation using the Recovery Console. The Windows 2000 Repair Options screen displays.

Press **C**, which starts the Recovery Console. Next, type **1** and press **Enter**. At the prompt, enter the administrator's password and press **Enter**.

The *C:\Winnt* command prompt appears. Type **cd ..** and press **Enter**. This changes to the root folder (C:\).

Type **copy Oldntldr Ntldr** at the command prompt and press **Enter**.

Type **exit** and press **Enter**. The computer reboots and should start normally.

Step 3

Log on to the system with the Administrator account.

Insert the Windows 2000 Professional CD into the CD-ROM drive. Close the Windows 2000 window when it displays.

Go to **Start** > **Run**, and in the box, type **D:\i386\winnt32** *[space]* **/cmdcons** and then click **OK**. The Windows 2000 Setup message box displays. *Note*: The CD-ROM drive letter might be different depending on the system's configuration.

Click **Yes** to install the Windows 2000 Recovery Console. Windows 2000 Setup installs the Windows 2000 Recovery Console to the hard disk.

Click **OK** to close the Setup dialog box.

Step 4

First, restart your computer, and at the boot loader menu, select **Microsoft Windows 2000 Recovery Console**.

The Windows 2000 Recovery Console starts up and prompts for the Windows 2000 installation to log on to. There should be only one choice to choose from at this point. Enter the administrator password when prompted and press **Enter**.

Type **help** and press **Enter** to see the list of available commands. Find the **Listsvc** command and use it to view all available services.

Type **Listsvc** at the command prompt (at the end of the list) and press **Enter** to view a list of available services. Press **Esc** to stop.

Type **disable /?** and press **Enter**. This command disables any Windows system service or driver.

Type **disable alerter** and press **Enter**.

The Alerter Service is now disabled. Note the lines of text advising that the Alerter Service has been changed. Type **exit** and press **Enter** to restart your computer. Boot into Windows 2000.

Now that you disabled the Alerter Service, you need to restart it.

Log on to the system with the Administrator account.

Next, navigate to the Computer Management window. The Computer Management window can be accessed in two ways:

Go to **Start** > **Programs** > **Administrative Tools** > **Computer Management**.

OR

Go to **Start** > **Settings** > **Control Panel** > **Administrative Tools** > **Computer Management**.

Next, expand Services And Applications by clicking the + sign and then click **Services**.

Double-click Alerter, change the Startup Type option to Automatic, and click **OK**.

Right-click Alerter, and click **Start**. Close the Computer Management window.

Troubleshooting

The Recovery Console is a useful tool when troubleshooting various problems. If the system stops responding or does not boot properly, it is a good place to go while troubleshooting the issue.

Reflection

Give an example of a problem that can be solved using the Recovery Console:

_____

_____

_____

_____

Lab 13.9.3: Windows Registry Backup and Recovery

Estimated Time: 20 Minutes

Objective

In this lab, you learn how to back up and perform a recovery of the Registry. These files are also referred to as the system state files.

Equipment

The following equipment is required for this exercise:

- Computer system running Windows 2000

Scenario

As the system administrator for the XYZ Company, a new software package is to be deployed onto a manager's system. This software has not been tested; however, you are aware that it will make changes to the Registry. The first step is making a backup of the system state files in case the software corrupts the system.

Procedures

The first step is to use the Windows Back Up Wizard to select the files that are to be backed up and then to perform the backup. Second, modify the Registry. It is possible that the system will not work after these changes to the Registry are made. Lastly, use the backup to restore the system state and Registry files.

Step 1

Log on to the server with the Administrator account.

When the systems boots up, go to **Start**, >**Run**.

In the Run dialog box, type **ntbackup** and click **OK**. The Backup dialog box should appear.

Take a minute to read the three options' descriptions under the Welcome tab, and then click the **Backup Wizard** button. The Backup Wizard should start.

Click **Next** to display the What To Back Up screen. Select the type of backup to be performed.

Click the **Only backup the System State Data** button, and click **Next**. At this point, the Where to Store the Backup screen displays. Select a place to save the file when prompted. This should be a predesignated folder for backup files.

The Completing The Backup Wizard screen should display. This screen shows the details of the backup that will be performed. At this point, additional changes can be made. Click the **Advanced** button.

When the Type Of Backup screen appears, make sure that **Normal** is selected and that the **Backup Migrated Remote Storage Data** check box is not checked.

Click **Next**. The How To Backup screen should display. Verify the backed up data after performing the backup.

Select the **Verify Data After Backup** check box, and click **Next**.

The Media Options page displays. Specify whether to **append this backup job to existing media** or **overwrite existing backup data on the destination media** at the prompt. Click the **Replace The Data On The Media With This Backup** button.

Click **Next**. Now the Backup Label screen displays. Supply a label for the backup job and for the backup media. Windows will supply a backup label and media label by using the current date and time by default.

In the Backup Label text box, type system state set created on **xxx**. (**xxx** is today's date and time.) Do not change anything in the Media Label text box; just click **Next**.

The When To Back Up screen displays. Choose whether to run the backup job now or schedule this backup job. For this lab, select the **Now** radio button. Click **Next**.

When the Completing The Backup Wizard screen displays, click **Finish** to start the backup job.

Windows Backup displays the Selection Information dialog box, which indicates the estimated amount of data for the backup and the time to complete it. Then, Windows Backup displays the Backup Progress dialog box, which shows the status of the backup operation, statistics on estimated and actual amount of data being processed, time that has elapsed, and estimated time that remains for the backup to complete.

When the backup is complete, click the **Report** button. A backup report displays. The backup report contains key details about the backup operation, such as the time it started and how many files were backed up. When finished, close Notepad.

Close the Backup Progress dialog box and the Backup Dialog box.

Step 2

Go to **Start** > **Run**. Type **Regedt32** in the box. The Registry Editor window should open.
Expand the **HKEY_LOCAL _MACHINE** Registry Key.

Right-click the **Hardware Folder**; select **Edit** and **Delete**.

Close the Registry Editor Box. The system is officially broken. In reality, only a virus would be able to damage the Registry like this. The point is that changes to your system can result in changes to the Registry. With the backup, the system can be restored.

Step 3

Locate the backup file that was saved in Step 1 of this lab.

Double-click that file. The Backup Utility Wizard displays.

Click the **Restore Wizard** button. The Welcome to the Restore Wizard screen displays. Click **Next**.

The What to Restore Wizard screen displays. Expand the file. Then, find the backup file that was created with the proper date and time and expand that. Click the **System State** check box. Click **Next**.

On the Completing the Restore Wizard screen, click **Advanced**.

On the Where to Restore screen, make sure that **original location** is selected. Click **Next**. If the Restoring System State will always overwrite files unless restored to a different location screen displays. Click **OK**.

Click the **Replace existing files if they are older than the backup files** radio button. Click **Next**.

Verify that all three radio buttons are selected and click **Next;** then click **Finish**.

The restore will begin by copying the files back to the system and by showing the progress results.

When the Restore Wizard completes, the report can be viewed by clicking the **Report** button. Click **Close**.

When prompted to restart your system, click **Yes**. Your system will restart.

Troubleshooting

Always back up the Registry when installing new software. If something is changed or removed in the Registry that affects the system, using the backup to fix it can save hours of troubleshooting.

Reflection

How can backing up the system state files save time?

_____

_____

_____

_____

Worksheet 13.4.5: Troubleshooting Software

Match each term with its description.

——	1. Clean Boot	A. A file that has a list of DOS statements that are executed when the computer is first started
——	2. Patch	B. An error that occurs when two programs that are running at the same time try to use the same area in memory
——	3. Boot Disk	C. Software that is still in the initial phase of testing within the software production house
——	4. Config.sys	D. A diagnostic state of Windows that allows you to fix problems that prevent you from starting Windows normally
——	5. Autoexec.bat	E. Software used to quick-fix a bug in a program
——	6. REM	F. Memory and hard drive space used by Windows
——	7. Safe Mode	G. A disk containing a rudimentary operating system that starts a computer
——	8. Registry	H. A way of starting a computer with a minimal set of drivers and programs
——	9. Device Manager	I. The second release of a program intended for the public, small selected group to test
——	10. Resources	J. A file that contains statements for loading memory drivers and that tells the operating system where key DOS files are located
——	11. GPF	K. A command that makes remarks in DOS startup files
——	12. Beta Release	L. Files that contain information about user settings and configuration information for applications
——	13. Alpha Release	M. A part of Windows that provides you with a visual presentation of physical devices in your system

Notes

Notes

Notes

Notes

Notes

Notes